The Archaeology of Bahrain
The British contribution

Proceedings of a seminar held on Monday 24th July 2000 to mark the exhibition 'Traces of Paradise' at the Brunei gallery, SOAS, London

Edited by

Harriet Crawford

BAR International Series 1189
2003

Published in 2016 by
BAR Publishing, Oxford

BAR International Series 1189

The Archaeology of Bahrain

ISBN 978 1 84171 555 1

© The editor and contributors severally and the Publisher 2003

The authors' moral rights under the 1988 UK Copyright,
Designs and Patents Act are hereby expressly asserted.

All rights reserved. No part of this work may be copied, reproduced, stored,
sold, distributed, scanned, saved in any form of digital format or transmitted
in any form digitally, without the written permission of the Publisher.

BAR Publishing is the trading name of British Archaeological Reports (Oxford) Ltd.
British Archaeological Reports was first incorporated in 1974 to publish the BAR
Series, International and British. In 1992 Hadrian Books Ltd became part of the BAR
group. This volume was originally published by Archaeopress in conjunction with
British Archaeological Reports (Oxford) Ltd / Hadrian Books Ltd, the Series principal
publisher, in 2003. This present volume is published by BAR Publishing, 2016.

Printed in England

BAR titles are available from:

	BAR Publishing
	122 Banbury Rd, Oxford, OX2 7BP, UK
EMAIL	info@barpublishing.com
PHONE	+44 (0)1865 310431
FAX	+44 (0)1865 316916
	www.barpublishing.com

In memory of Martin Hicks 1961-1999

Foreword
by
Sir John Hanson, Chairman of Trustees,
The Bahrain-British Foundation

The papers in this volume were given at a seminar "The Archaeology of Bahrain: the British contribution" which was sponsored by The Bahrain-British Foundation and held at the School of Oriental and African Studies, London, on Monday 24th July 2000. The Foundation acknowledges a debt of gratitude to Dr. Harriet Crawford of the Institute of Archaeology for convening the Seminar for us so meticulously and to the School for its generosity in providing the venue. Our thanks are also due to Ms Jan Picton who recorded the talks and later transcribed them to form the basis of the published articles. To be precise the venue was the excellent Brunei Gallery, within the School, which was at the time playing host to the beautifully presented exhibition "Traces of Paradise" which unfolded the story of Bahrain's early history. It was the exhibition, organised by the Dilman Committee under the chairmanship of Michael Rice, advisor to The Bahrain-British Foundation, that provided the inspiration and the context for the Seminar.

The British contribution to the archaeology of Bahrain goes back far more than a century and is substantial. The ten seasons of expeditions led by Dr. Killick, Dr. Moon and Dr. Crawford represent the latest, and distinguished, contribution within that tradition. At the suggestion of Bahraini colleagues it was decided to dedicate the Seminar to the memory of the archaeologist Martin Hicks who spent many years in Bahrain as Assistant Director of the London-Bahrain Archaeological Expendition and who tragically lost his life there while he was a member of the team working at Saar.

The Bahrain-British Foundation is very pleased to have been involved actively with the Seminar and to be associated with this volume. The Foundation was established over ten years ago on the initiative of the two governments as an educational charity which provides opportunities for young people in Bahrain and Britain to spend up to a year in the other country for educational and cultural purposes. The Trustees have always believed that history and archaeology are important fields for the Foundation to support and that is what brought the Seminar and the Foundation together.

List of contributors:

Dr Robert Carter. Institute of Archaeology, University College London

Dr Harriet Crawford. Institute of Archaeology, University College London

Dr Robert Killick. Director, London-Bahrain Archaeological Expedition

Michael Rice. Hon. Secretary Bahrain-British Foundation.

Professor Michael Roaf. University of Munich. Germany

Dr Archie Walls. FSA. Giles Quarme & Associates

Contents

The British Contribution to the archaeology of Bahrain: the early years
Michael Rice 1

Excavations at al-Markh
Michael Roaf 7

Dilmun at the turn of the millennium: living at Saar
Robert Killick 13

Diraz East and A'ali East
Michael Roaf 25

Restructuring Bronze Age trade: Bahrain, southeast Asia and the copper question
Robert Carter 31

Arad fort: its restoration and foreign relations
Archie Walls 43

Bibliography 61

Postscript
Harriet Crawford 65

List of Illustrations

Frontispiece
Colour plate 'Bahrain: land of living waters' Watercolour by Thomas Mitchell
Map. The Bahrain islands showing the sites mentioned in the text (J.Picton)

Michael Rice: The British Contribution to the archaeology of Bahrain: the early years

Colour plate: Top 'War Bugulours laid up on the shore' Thomas Mitchell
           Bottom ' Ruin of a Portugese fort' Thomas Mitchell
a. Drawing of a fish Captain E.I.Durand
b. Drawing of an A'ali mounds. Durand
c. Blocking of an entrance to one of the mounds
d. Interior of A'ali mound. Durand
e. Inscribed stone foot found by Durand
f. Theodore Bent at A'ali

Michael Roaf: Excavations at al-Markh

Fig.a. Sketchmap. The location of Al Markh in Ubaid times
Fig.b. East section of trench J19 at Al Markh
Fig.c. Chart showing distribution of of finds from trench J19 in earlier and later periods
Fig.d. Chart showing the distribution of the major fish groups from trench J19
Fig.e. Great salmon catfish otolith
Fig.f. Chart showing approximate food contribution of the most common edible shells
Fig.g. Bi-facial Arrowheads
Fig.h. Ubaid painted pottery

Robert Killick: Dilmun at the turn of the millennium: living at Saar

Figure 1   Schematic plan of Saar
Figure 2   The settlement and plain from the air.
Figure 3   A row of identical buildings
Figure 4   A Standard A-Series Building (Bldg 226).
Figure 5   Standard installations (a) Jar support with plastered trough
             (b) Coned jar support (c) Tannur
Figure 6   Plan of Bldg 56
Figure 7   Plastered rooms in Bldg 56
Figure 8   Gypsum kiln
Figure 9   The Temple from the air.
Figure 10 Bitumen beads.

Michael Roaf: **Diraz East and A'ali East**

Plate

Plans of the excavations at Diraz East before (a) and after (b) the reconstruction.

Fig.a. Stamp seal of Early Dilmun type from Room 5 at Diraz East.

Fig.b. The temple after reconstruction

Fig.c. Stamp seal from Tomb (6) at Diraz East

Fig.d. General view of Tombs B and A at A'ali East

Fig.e. Mesopotamian Cylinder seal from Tomb A at A'ali East

Fig.f. 'Persian Gulf' stamp seal from Tomb A at A'ali East

Fig.g. Middle Dilmun two sided stamp seal from Tomb A at A'ali East

Fig.h. Early Dilmun seal from a pit dug into Tomb B at A'ali East

Robert Carter: **Restructuring Bronze Age trade: Bahrain, southeast Asia and the copper question**

Fig.a. Chronological table

Fig.b. Map of major routes and sites (adapted from Potts.T. 1994 fig.5)

Fig.c. Map of copper and tin sources (adapted from Potts.T. 1994 fig.21)

Archie Walls: **Arad fort: its restoration and foreign relations**

1. Demonstracao da ilha de Baren circa 1635.
2. Excavations carried out by Dr M.Kevran
3. Construction principles
4. Plan of the lower areas
5. Plan of the upper areas
6. Original construction of a bastion: inner fortifications
7. The estuary and its channel: fields of fire
8. Reconstruction of the south bastion
9. South bastion: plan of upper areas
10. sectional perspective showing the moat and the ramp.
11. Inner entrance: SW elevation
12. Inner entrance: restored SW elevation
13. Inner entrance NE elevation
14. Inner entrance: restored NE elevation
15. The entrance vault: reconstruction sequence

Colour plate: Arad fort before (a) and after (b) restoration

The colour illustrations in this volume have been produced with the financial assistance of the Bahrain-British Foundation

Colour plate 'Bahrain: land of living waters' Watercolour by Thomas Mitchell

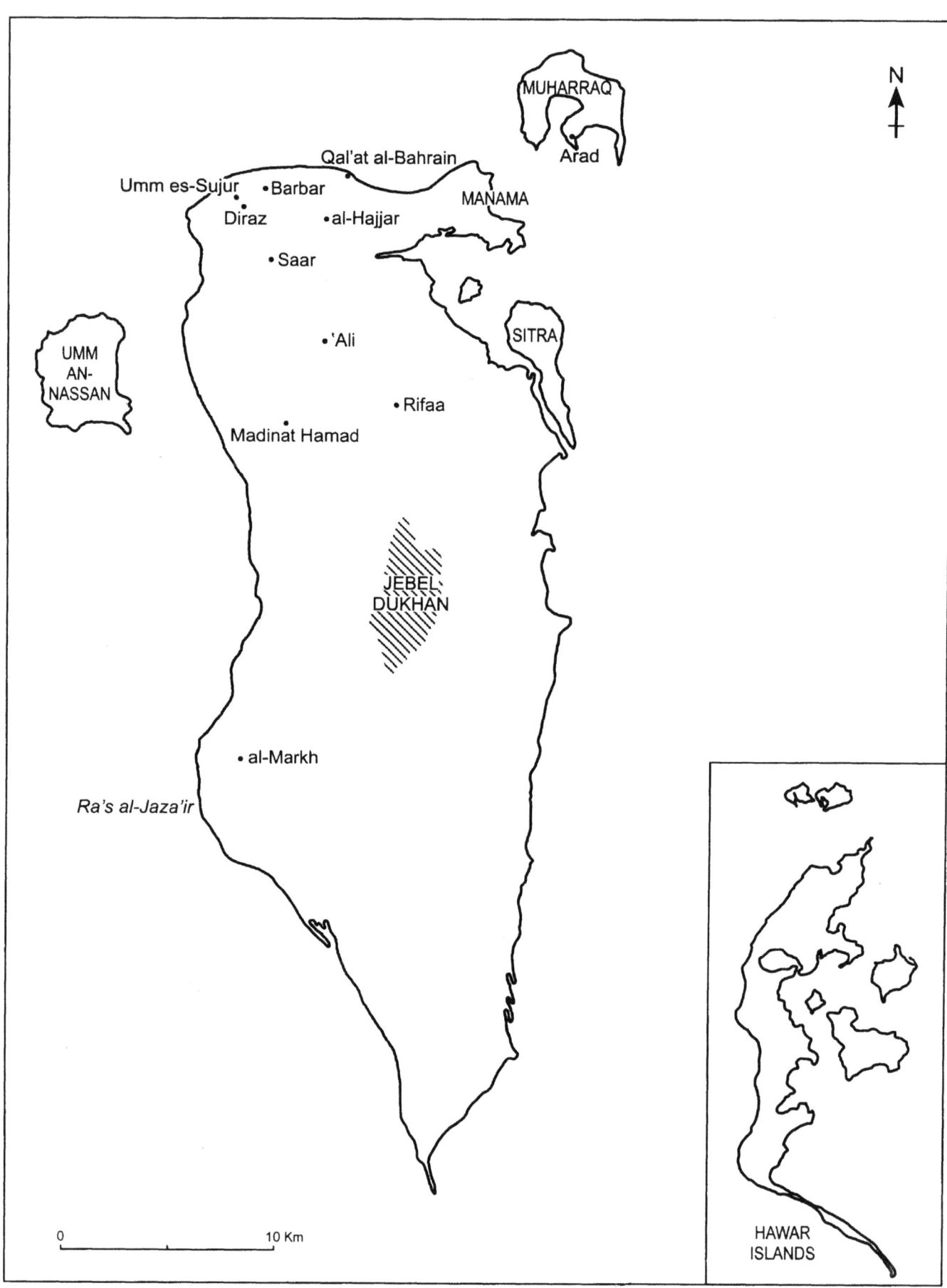

Map. The Bahrain islands showing the sites mentioned in the text (J. Picton)

THE BRITISH CONTRIBUTION TO THE ARCHAEOLOGY OF BAHRAIN : THE EARLY YEARS

Michael RICE

The British, or more precisely the English, connection with Bahrain and the Gulf goes back to the seventeenth century, though the interests represented in earlier days were generally far from scholarly. The earliest travellers of note were the Shirley brothers who, four centuries ago, in 1600, went to Persia with the purpose of setting up a trading relationship with London. They evidently visited or at least were in contact with Bahrain, the source of highly prized pearls.

The next expedition of relevance was military, an excursion prompted by Britain's burgeoning Imperial interests and the perceived need to secure the routes to India, when in 1809\10 English troops razed the Al-Qasimi stronghold at Ras Al-Khaima, the occasion for the production of a famous series of drawings by Lieutenant Temple, later made into prints and published in London in1816, of the attack on the town's fortress [Temple 1913]. The scenes are dramatic but the events must have done little to commend the British to the inhabitants of the Gulf. Treaties with the Shaikhs of the Gulf followed and in 1820 a 'General Treaty of Peace' was signed by various of the rulers of the states, including Bahrain, with the first Anglo-Bahraini Agreement being concluded in 1861 when the formal relationship between the Ruler of Bahrain and the British Crown was confirmed.

The first evidence of interest in the antiquities of Bahrain, though they were not yet described as such, came as a result of a visit to the islands in the mid-nineteenth century by the elder of two brothers, both artists, Thomas and William Frederick Mitchell. Thomas, the elder, was a naval architect and both he and his brother were, in the manner of the time, very competent draughtsmen; indeed, William Frederick became a successful professional artist, despite disabilities from which he had suffered since childhood. Thomas seems to have spent some six months in Bahrain and produced a group of very evocative and appealing water-colour paintings of scenes around the islands, in the interior as well as at coastal locations. It is likely that Thomas made these drawings during voyages that he undertook, first whilst serving on the Cape and East Indies Station in 1864-5 and again in 1870-3.

The paintings were entirely unknown until 1987 when they surfaced in Phillips' saleroom in Par, Cornwell, near the Mitchell family's home [Phillips catalogue 1987]. Fortunately, it was possible for the paintings to be acquired for the Government of Bahrain though, less fortunately perhaps, several different interests were bidding and, in consequence, the prices were very considerably above the admittedly modest estimates which the auctioneers had set.

The paintings show vividly how Bahrain looked before European influences became dominant. It is however not difficult to recognise the areas painted by Thomas Mitchell, including what were the first pictorial records of some of the monuments, notably the site of the Qala'at al-Bahrain, and what was probably the first reference to the fields of grave mounds since classical times, though here they are disguised as the ruins of the 365 towns which were said to have to have been on 'the island of Barhein' (sic). The following descriptions are based on the entries in the catalogue of the sale from which the drawings were acquired. Mitchell's spellings and punctuation have been retained in the transcriptions of his annotations.

A number of the paintings have been annotated by the artist, sometimes extensively. This is the case with a study of 'a palm-fringed pool and irrigation channel' (Frontispiece). There are three separate captions on the obverse of the painting. On the left hand side: *"There should appear on this bank a troop of donkeys and the attendant boys – but the artist found it rather warm to complete the picture and therefore dived into........"* beneath the picture.... *"The Pool" Barhein Persian Gulf – reservoir 28ft. deep made by heaping earth around a spring and then building and facing it, it irrigates the Date gardens for many miles around. Here we bathed every evening during the hot season – the water retains the heat of 80° (about) all the year round – in the winter the water seems disagreeably warm, in the summer it is beautifully cool,"* on the right hand side .... *"Here we used to float about smoke our pipes and eat figs – there are many fish but not good to eat. Men suffering from heat apoplexy found much relief at living at this pool –The air being dryer than over the sea which was 96°".*

'A lake with palm fringed shores' is annotated *"Date-gardens, Barhein Persian Gulf – In these gardens almonds and many other things are grown – irrigation is produced by reservoirs built around springs, the water being conveyed by ditches".*

An extensive annotation appears on a landscape drawing inscribed *"One of the 365 – Barhein"* and annotated *"It is said that there were once 365 towns on the island of Barhein. It is probable that there were many, for at many places scatterd over the islands are collections of mounds which cover much ground – the buildings are mostly of mud or clay baked only in the sun which would soon be reduced to mounds by the action of sun and moon"* and separately *"Supposed ruin of a town - Barhein Persian Gulf"*. On the reverse of the painting is another landscape annotated *"View with your back turned to the Pool".*

Another, described as a shore scene with a town, figures and boats, (Colour plate:top) is inscribed *"Barhein. War*

'War Bugulours laid up on the shore' (Thomas Mitchell)

'Ruin of a Portugese fort' (Thomas Mitchell)

Bugalours laid up" and annotated *"Barhein – Persian Gulf – With War Bugalours laid up according to Treaty"*.

The Qala'at al-Bahrain is illustrated in a drawing (Colour plate: Bottom) described in the catalogue as 'Landscape with ruins in the background' and captioned *"Ruin of a Portuguese Fort – Barhein Persian Gulf – within are two wells, very deep, one of which is filled up – it is surmounted by very high Date-gardens"*. A painting of 'a landscape with a distant fort' (the Qala'at) is annotated *"The Fort at Barhein – Persian Gulf"*. Another study of ruins is inscribed "Ruins of Village and Mosque Barhein" .

Altogether, Thomas Mitchell's painting represent a most valuable archive of mid-nineteenth century Bahrain.

Rather more than thirty years later, the arrival of a visitor with an overtly scholarly interest in Bahrain is recorded. This was the now celebrated visit which Captain E.L.Durand, Assistant Political Resident at Bushire, made to the islands on behalf of the Foreign Office of the Viceroy of India in the winter of 1878\79. Accompanied by a troop of Sepoys and with the company of a bull terrier puppy, Captain Durand spent six months in Bahrain, copiously noting the evidence of ancient settlements and recording a good deal of what today might be considered anthropological information about the life of the people and the environment of the islands. It has been suggested that Captain Durand's interest was not confined purely to academic or scholarly pursuits - that he was, in effect, spying, though what he would have been spying on is not clear to me.

Durand's report, made to the office of the Viceroy in Calcutta, is a fascinating document, not only for the mass of information about contemporary Bahrain and its antiquities which it contains but also for its form. It exists in two versions; the first [Durand 1879], prepared for his colleagues in the Viceregal service, is chatty, discursive, in parts rather oddly, a trifle winsome. The second [Durand 1880], much more formal, is the text of a lecture which he gave in London in November 1879 to the Royal Asiatic Society.

His report to the Viceroy's office is enlivened with a series of most engaging drawings of antiquities, the mounds, fauna, including a fish which he describes as wearing an overcoat (Fig.a), and the flora of Bahrain. He excavated several mounds at 'Aali, and he drew details of their construction and of their interiors (Fig.b/c/d); he describes his methods of excavation and, in the manner of the day, was not above dynamiting inconvenient walls or obtrusive rocks. In this he

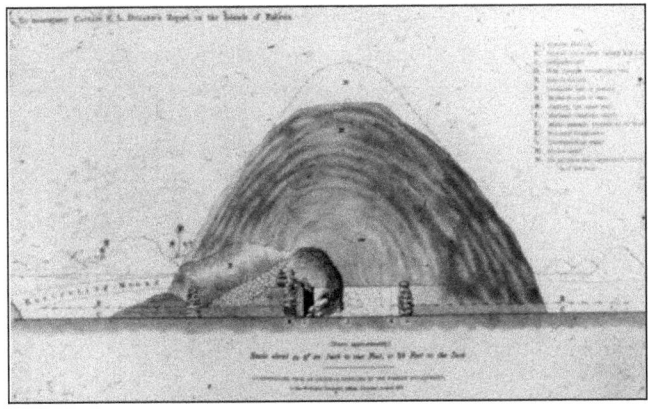

Fig. b. Drawing of an A'ali mounds. (Durand)

Fig. c. Blocking of an entrance to one of the mounds

Fig. d. Interior of A'ali mound. (Durand)

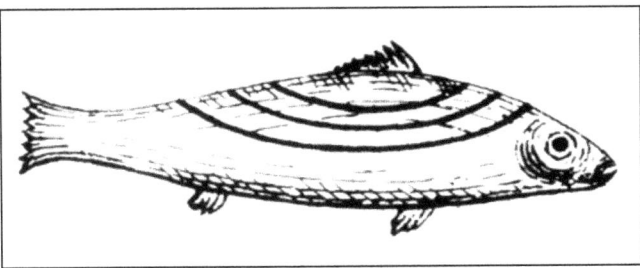

Fig. a. Drawing of a fish Captain E.I. (Durand)

was following common practice. After all, only a comparatively few years before Colonel Howard-Vyse had used the same refinement of technique when investigating the Pyramid of Khnum-Khufu at Giza. There he blew open the principal entrance to the pyramid on its north face. The results of his work can be seen to this day.

Durand was an extremely perceptive observer. He recognised two large worked blocks of stone on the site which nearly a hundred years later was to be identified by the Danish Expedition as the important early second millennium temple of Barbar. The two blocks represented the entrance to the third temple, on its north face.

His return to London provided the opportunity for him to address the Royal Asiatic Society at a meeting in November 1880 at a meeting in Burlington House at which the President and Director of the Society, Sir Henry Rawlinson, provided a commentary of exceptional erudition [Rawlinson 1880]. He it was who, as a young army officer, had climbed the sheer face of the rocks at Behistun to copy the trilingual inscription, which eventually led to the translation of Sumerian cuneiform. In his commentary to Durand's paper he confirmed the opinion of the French savant, Oppert, that the Bahrain islands were the location of the Sumerians' mystical land of Dilmun.

Durand made one significant and celebrated discovery, the inscribed stone block which he found embedded in the wall of a mosque on the island, at Bilad ed-Kadim. This bore the name of the god Inzak who was later to be recognised as the tutelary divinity of Dilmun and as the son of the Sumerian god of the Abyss, Enki, Ea in the Old Babylonian language of the inscription (Fig.e).

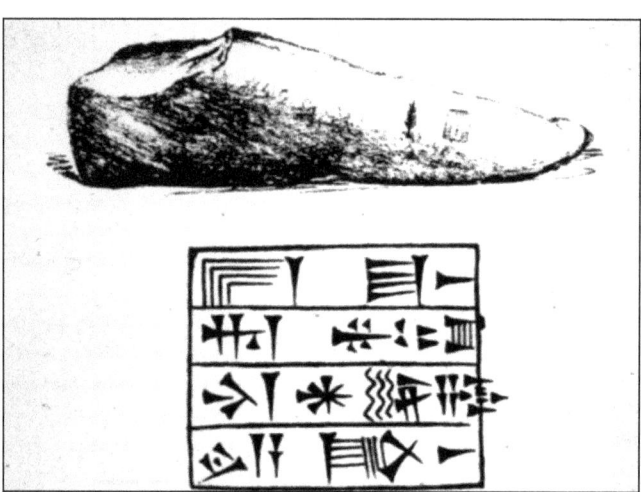

Fig. e. Inscribed stone foot found by Durand

Durand lived to a distinguished old age, dying a baronet and a Major General. He was the author of the very authentically entitled 'With Rifle, Rod and Spear in the East'. He died at his house in Ennismore Gardens, in Knightsbridge in London which was bombed during the Second World War, resulting in the loss of the inscribed stone. Durand had removed it from Bahrain and brought it home with him as a trophy of his time in the islands. However, if it had not been for the drawing which he made of the stone and its inscription for his report to the Viceroy's office, there would be no evidence of this most important document in the archaeology of Bahrain.

Like Thomas Mitchell, Durand was a talented draughtsman and water-colourist. Many of his drawings of sites in Afghanistan are kept in the archives of the British Library but sadly none of those which it is reasonable to suppose he must have produced from his Bahrain visit are in the Library's holdings. I have enquired of his surviving family but they know of no paintings from what was the first serious attempt to chart the monuments and early history of the islands.

The next event in the history of Bahrain's archaeology with British connections was a lecture given by J. Theodore Bent, an American traveller and author, to the Royal Geographical Society in London who with his wife visited Bahrain in 1890 [Bent 1890]. This created a considerable degree of interest, rather more, indeed than had Durand's lecture and publication a decade earlier. In the discussion of Bent's paper, in which he described the opening of one of the grave-mounds at Aali, the British Museum expressed some enthusiasm for Bent's findings, to the extent of offering a subvention of £100 for further exploration in the island. Despite the suggestion that Bahrain might have been the *To Nefer*, the primeval holy land of the ancient Egyptians – a suggestion put forward by Mr Cecil Smith of the Museum – this generous proposal was not followed up. The material which Bent excavated is said to have been handed to the British Museum. His wife, Mrs Anne Bent, who after her husband's death published 'South Arabia', a record of their journeys, a book which is notable for the lively and engaging portrait which it gives of life in Bahrain and of the court of the long-living Ruler, Shaikh Isa bin Ali Al-Khalifa and for the sometimes breathless quality of her descriptive style. There is a splendid photograph of Theodore Bent, dressed more appropriately for grouse-shooting on a Yorkshire moor than for the deserts of Bahrain, at Aali in the company of a number of Bahraini dignitaries (Fig.f).

Fig. f. Theodore Bent at A'ali

British political representatives abroad have always been known for their interest in, and sympathy with, the past of the countries in which they served. Sometimes, as may have been the case with Durand, concerns other than the strictly scholarly have been attributed to them, but following the precedent of Durand, who was an Assistant Political Resident, the Political Resident of thirty years later himself carried out what was effectively the first scientific study of the monuments of Bahrain. This was Colonel F.B. Prideaux and he conducted a thorough survey of the monuments of Aali (Figs 12.13), in particular, in 1905. He mapped the mounds and produced a detailed plan of the 'Royal Tombs' (Fig.14), as well as a carefully documented map of the island overall. He also published a fascinating study of topographical terms and place names of Bahrain and the adjacent Arabian mainland, drawing on the work of the Arab lexicographer Yakut, which, at the time, was very little known. His report was published in the Archaeological Survey of India [Prideaux 1912], its text slightly marred by topographical errors which suggest that it was proof-read by someone to whom English was not a native tongue.

The next British initiative came from Flinders Petrie, the Father, as he is sometimes called, of British Egyptology. He was a man, in the manner of his time, of immense and universal enthusiasms. Very early on in his career, in the early 1890's, when he was frustrated at not being able to get at the royal burials at Abydos, he considered digging in Bahrain as a possibility. One of his enduring preoccupations, to which he returned not infrequently in the course of an active career which spanned some seventy years, was that the dynastic Egyptians came to the Nile Valley from southwestern Asia via 'the islands of the Persian Gulf'. Whilst this idea would find little scholarly support today, there is no doubt that there is very significant if enigmatic evidence of influences from southwestern Iran and Sumer in late predynastic and early dynastic Egypt and Petrie was right to recognise them.

Petrie explored the connections between late predynastic Egypt, southwest Asia and the Gulf, on several occasions throughout his career. In 1917, in the journal *Ancient Egypt* which he himself published, in an article entitled 'The Geography of the Gods', he wrote "The movement of the dynastic people appears to have been by sea, round from the Persian Gulf and up the Red Sea into Egypt."[Petrie 1917]

In 1926, again in *Ancient Egypt* he explored the presence in late predynastic Egypt of many design motifs which could only have originated in Mesopotamia and south west Asia. He observed "The probability seems that they ['people of Elamite or Tigrian origins and ideas'] had branched off to some settlement in the Persian Gulf (such as the Bahreyn islands)..." [Petrie 1926]

He returned to this same theme at the end of his life in his last book, *The Making of Egypt* [Petrie 1939]. It is only in comparatively recent years that Egyptologists have come to recognise the significance of these foreign influences on the development of the historic culture of the Nile Valley.

Petrie sought to encourage T.E. Lawrence [Drower 1985], who was an archaeologist before he became a creature of myth as a result of his engagements in Arabia during the First World War, to go to Bahrain to investigate the possibility of wider connections as suggested by the evidence which Durand and Bent had reported. Lawrence was intrigued and because of the relationship with Britain remarked, in a letter to friend, regarding whatever material might be excavated, 'I suppose we might carry off the stuff' [Lawrence ?]. Before he could make a decision war loomed and he discovered another and perhaps more appropriate destiny.

Petrie intervened again when he persuaded E. J. Mackay, one of his protégés from his work in Egypt, to spend a season in Bahrain. This Mackay did in 1925, publishing the results of his work in the now very rare volume, *Bahrain and Hammamieh* [Mackay et al. 1929], in the series published under the auspices of the British School of Archaeology in Egypt. His report is really the first full scale scholarly study of the antiquities of Bahrain, other than that produced by Colonel Prideaux for the Archaeological Survey of India in 1907. Mackay did a service to professional archaeology by producing a number of excellent photographs of the excavations of the mounds which he conducted (ill.16), drawings of pottery and a study of the design motifs which appeared on them. He was however, misled, as others had been before him, into believing that the occasional ivory pieces found in the tombs were attributable to the Phoenicians. It was from his excavations that the ivory figurine of a naked female (Fig.16 came to the British Museum. Mackay was later to be one of the pioneers of the archaeology of the Indian sub-continent.

In 1928, shortly after Mackay's visit, a remarkable linguistic study by E. J. Burrows SJ, was published in the papers of the Biblical Pontifical Institute of Rome [Burrows 1928], a work of almost overwhelming erudition, which examined the possibility that Dilmun-Bahrain represented the idea of the Terrestrial Paradise to the Sumerians. His report is handwritten, illuminated by different coloured inks for the various languages and epigraphies with which he fills it. He attempts to analyse the meaning of the name 'Dilmun' and produces a series of interpretations which I suspect few scholars would support today. It is however, a most intriguing document.

In 1933 Professor C.J.Gadd published a seminal article [Gadd 1932] on seals from the Gulf, which had been found at Ur where Burrows was epigrapher. This was the first record of one of the most typical artefacts from the Dilmun civilisation and which, over the years, have received considerable attention from scholars.

After the Second World War the British connection was maintained through the work of an English archaeologist, Geoffrey Bibby, who will always be associated with the successive Danish Expeditions, supported by the Bahrain Government, the Bahrain Oil Company and the Carlsberg Foundation, in the 1950s, 60s, and 70s. The Danish Expeditions, led by Bibby after Professor P.V. Glob, the original leader, withdrew from active involvement on the ground, advanced the archaeology of Bahrain to international status and recognition, to the point where Dilmun was recognised as one of the cultures of the Bronze Age which, like its contemporaries in Mesopotamia, Egypt and the Levant, is directly ancestral to the world of today [Bibby 19??].

In 1970 the Danish Expedition was instrumental in bringing to Bahrain The Third International Conference in Asian Archaeology. The Conference was attended by a distinguished representative group of archaeologists concerned with its subject, including the very few, other than the Danes, who were involved with Arabian archaeology – or indeed had heard of it. The Conference was the occasion for the design and installation of the first Bahrain National Museum, which was located in the newly erected Government House in the capital, Manama (Fig.17). The work was carried out by a British consultancy, which had also been involved with the organisation of the Conference, working with the members of the Danish Expedition, especially Bibby.

Amongst those attending the Conference were several of the luminaries of British archaeology of the day. These included Sir Mortimer Wheeler, the first Director of the Institute of Archaeology and then Secretary of the British Academy, Sir Lawrence Kirwan, of the Royal Geographical Society, Dame Kathleen Kenyon, who had excavated extensively in Jerusalem and Dr Richard Barnett, the Keeper of Western Asiatic Antiquities at the British Museum. With others who were of a like mind, these distinguished authorities felt that a British involvement in the archaeology of Bahrain should be encouraged and British institutions urged to participate in what was clearly, as revealed by the Conference, likely to become a most rewarding field for research and active involvement on the ground.

Meeting in the elegant surroundings of the British Academy at Burlington House London, it was agreed to form *The Committee for East Arabia and the Gulf*, first under Wheeler's chairmanship and later that of Richard Barnett, which was to spearhead British scholarly interests in Bahrain. Later, it was also to provide assistance to the newly emerging archaeological services which were beginning to be set up in the Arabian peninsula states. The Committee was subsequently renamed The Society for Arabian Studies and its work continues to this day.

Nearly fourteen years after this Conference another was held in Bahrain in December 1983, on the occasion of the 200th Anniversary of the arrival of the Al-Khalifa family and their supporters in the Bahrain islands. In 1970 seven papers were presented which bore on archaeology; thirteen years later over a hundred papers relating specifically to Bahrain were discussed by the one hundred and thirty-plus scholars who attended the Conference. Under the title 'Bahrain Through the Ages', it was organised by British consultants working in close connection with the Ministry of Information of the Kingdom of Bahrain. After the Conference, two substantial volumes of proceedings were edited and published in London containing eighty-nine of the papers discussed at the Conference, which have now become standard works of reference [al Khalifa & Rice 1986, 1993].

Amateurs have also played their part in uncovering the archaeology of Bahrain. One of these, a British officer named Higham, serving in Bahrain, opened a tomb of the Hellenistic period and found some notable artefacts of which two particularly fine pieces of glass (Figs 18,19) are now in the British Museum. [During-Caspers 1980, Exhibition Catalogue 2000] They, like Mackay's ivory statuette, had been taken into the British Museum's collections, in the days before the antiquities of Bahrain, like those of so many other countries, were protected by legislation designed to prevent unauthorised excavation.

The latest contribution which Britain has made to the archaeology of Bahrain has been the ten seasons conducted at the site of the thus far unique Bronze Age settlement at Saar [Crawford at al.1997, Crawford 1998].The work at Saar has written a new chapter in the history of Bahrain. Unlike so many studies of the ancient world which concern themselves almost exclusively with the lives and achievements of the Great Ones of the past, Saar has thrown a warm and kindly light on the lives of ordinary people, living in Bahrain four thousand years ago, concerned with making a living for themselves and their families in a little town, dominated by its temple, as today you might find a town of comparable size, nestling round its mosque or village church.

I am proud to claim a very small part in this phase of Britain's contribution to the archaeology of Bahrain for I was introduced to the site after the Jordanian teams that had worked there in the 1980s had withdrawn. It was obvious – even to me – that it was a site which would repay further work and which urgently required protection. I was keen to see British archaeologists working in Bahrain and I described the site and what seemed to me to be its potential to John Shepherd, the then newly appointed British Ambassador to Bahrain. He immediately saw the importance of the site and secured the support – including ultimately the financial support, itself no mean achievement- of the British government. By a happy chance, at the same time Dr Killick and Dr Moon had been invited to visit Bahrain, with Dr Crawford, to investigate the possibility of obtaining a permit to excavate. They of course recognised the importance of Saar and the result was the London-Bahrain Expedition, a partnership between British and Bahraini archaeologists under the patronage of the Ministry of Information (now the Ministry of Cabinet Affairs and Information) and the Institute of Archaeology, University of London.

It is surely gratifying for those of us of British nationality, to reflect that scholars from our own country have been able to play an enduring part, extending for one hundred and twenty years, in uncovering the rich heritage of a country with which we have had so long and friendly a connection, from a part of the world of such historic importance about which so little was known for so long.

BRITISH EXCAVATIONS AT AL MARKH

Michael ROAF

The British Archaeological Expedition to Bahrain, which worked between 1973 and 1978, was set up after a conference held in Bahrain in 1970 where Sir Mortimer Wheeler, amongst other people, decided that it would be a good idea for British archaeologists to be involved in Bahrain. In the autumn of 1973 Tony McNicoll and David Oates went out for a preliminary visit to the island, in the course of which they looked at a large number of sites. One of these was the site of Al Markh, which had been identified by amateur archaeologists in Bahrain. It had pottery and flint on the surface that were recognisable as being considerably earlier than most of the known monuments on the islands. These belong mainly to the so-called Early Dilmun, or Barbar Period, with which most of the papers in this volume are concerned. I want to describe the remains of an earlier period, about 4000 BC, which up until then had been a blank in the island of Bahrain.

In the late 1960s and the early 1970s pottery was discovered in the eastern province of Arabia and in Qatar which could be dated to the 5th millennium BC. (Bibby 1972) This was a very interesting discovery. Before this there had been no indication that there had been any connections with Mesopotamia at this early period. Suddenly, a whole rash of sites was discovered in eastern Arabia which produced pottery sherds decorated in a style which could be identified with the Ubaid culture of Mesopotamia. The site that Tony McNicoll investigated on Bahrain (Roaf 1976) was on the west coast of the island, south of Zallaq, near a BAPCO oil company road. (Map) It was given the number 2027 and was called Al Markh because the nearest name on the map was an area about 2 km to the north-east labelled Al Markh.

The site is a low sandy mound which is hardly visible, but on the surface Tony McNicoll found various flint tools, including arrow-heads, some fish-bones and a few sherds of pottery, some of them painted. He decided to carry out a short sondage in the winter of 1973/4 with results that showed that the site was worth further investigation. Today Al Markh lies some distance from the sea, almost 1.5 km from the present coastline, but in the 5th millennium BC it seems to have been part of an island lying off the main coast of Bahrain (Fig. a).

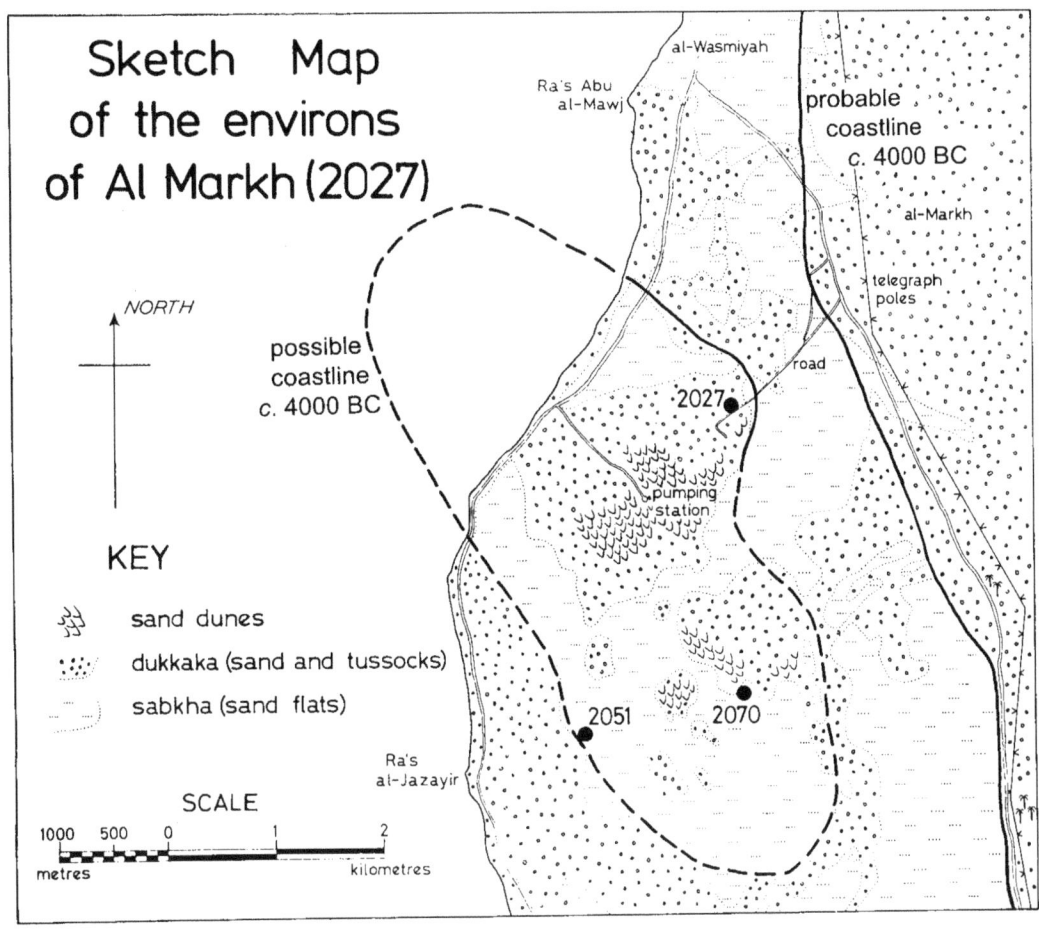

Fig.a. Sketchmap. The location of Al Markh in Ubaid times

There is no obvious water supply, although we did discover that if you dig at the base of the sand-dunes you can get fresh water. There is another similarly dated site close by with just a scatter of flint and a few potsherds (site 2070), and at Ra's al-Jazayir (site 2051), not far away, there is the shell-mound dating to a slightly later period which was excavated by the Danish team (Nielson 1958).

Tony McNicoll opened four different trenches in his first season. In the following year he was appointed Director of the British Institute in Afghanistan and I was asked to take over the excavations in Bahrain. I thought I was going out to dig a Barbar period second millennium temple at Diraz, but there were problems with the land ownership and we were diverted to continue work at Al Markh. We excavated two trenches in 1975, one of which, J19, is the subject of this paper.

The trench measured about 6m by 6m and had a depth of about 1m or so, with various rather indistinctly differentiated layers of sand and ashy sand. In the course of our work we distinguished early on that there was a major change about half way down, between the upper layers and the lower layers. The upper layers were mainly of drifted sand; in the lower, much darker layers, there were lenses with lots of fish-bone in, and right at the bottom were several shallow pits dug into the natural sand which seemed to have been the bases of hearths or fire-pits. (Fig. b)

In the lowest part of the excavation we came across a deposit, about 35cm deep in places, which was literally solid with fish-bones. The bone was in a fairly fragile condition. We had been sieving the rest of the site with a 4mm wire sieve, but that would have just crushed the fish-bones to powder.

Fig.b. East section of trench J19 at Al Markh

We gathered the earth together in rubber buckets and spent some happy afternoons in the sea wet-sieving the remains of these layers in plastic fly-screen mesh of about 1.5mm with the result that we collected a rather large sample of small fish-bones.

To summarise: basically the site of Al Markh had two main periods, a later phase, and an earlier phase. In terms of volume of earth excavated there is approximately the same amount of earth – 14 cu.m. in the later phase, 12 cu.m. in the earlier phase – but there was a very different distribution of finds within these phases (Fig. c). Within the lower phase there were various layers, some that were more sandy, some that were darker, and the midden which was solid with fish-bones. In the analysis we sometimes distinguished these because it seems that the sandy layers drifted in whereas the darker layers and the midden are actual deposits in-situ. The fish-bone is one of the most interesting aspects of the site because it has recently been studied by Angela von den Driesch and Henriette Manhart from Munich University and they have written a very extensive report on the subject (Driesch and Manhart 2000)

From the enormous number of fish bones from the site more than 140,000 fish-bones have now been looked at. There are a lot of bones in a fish but looking at so many bones is fairly remarkable. About 120,000 of them are not identifiable, but more than 16,000 bones were identified either to family or, in many cases, to species. The majority of the fish come from the lower layers where more than 130,000 bones were examined.

Some 30 different species were identified in this analysis, some of them by a single example so that one bone in 130,000 bones has given evidence that that species was present. Obviously such fish did not contribute significantly to the diet of the inhabitants of the site and I want to concentrate mainly on the more frequently occurring fish. It is a little difficult to talk about fish-bone statistically because there are many factors that affect the preservation of fish-bones. Sharks and other cartilaginous fish do not have any true bones, they have a skeleton made of cartilage which is sometimes preserved when it is calcified, but most of the skeletal elements just do not survive in the archaeological record. Some fish have very easily identified bones, while others are much more difficult to identify, and our interpretation of the bones is based on the evidence that is preserved and on our ability to identify it. The figures given below need not necessarily be the proportions that were originally present on the site or the proportion of the different types of fishes that were caught there.

	Volume excavated	Fish bone	Mammal bone	Number of shells	Most common edible shells	Flint chips	Pottery sherds
Later Phase	14.17 cu.m.	abundant poor preservation	abundant goat	4427	pearl oyster and murex	6003 22.27 kg	8
Earlier Phase	11.92 cu.m.	very abundant good preservation	very rare	2533	pearl oyster and venus clams	674 2.77 kg	143

Fig. c. Distribution of finds from trench J19 in the Later and Earlier phases.

Fish family and common name	Al Markh J19 Later	%	J19 Earlier	%	Saar Temple	%	Qala'at al-Bahrain	%	Shimal	%
Dorosomidae Gizzard-shads	0	0.0	1,434	8.	0	0.	0	0.	0	0.
Serranidae Groupers	157	57.7	444	2.	99	9.	1,041	35.9	21	1.
Carangidae Trevallies and Jacks	8	2.9	20	0.	72	7.	428	14.8	770	36.0
Gerres and *Leiognathus* Slimies and Silver-biddies	0	0.0	430	2.	0	0.	0	0.	0	0.
Lethrinidae Emperors	8	2.9	259	1.	380	37.0	888	30.6	18	0.
Sparidae Sea Breams	96	35.3	13,470	83.2	216	21.0	450	15.5	260	12.2
Sphyraenidae Barracudas	0	0.0	23	0.	190	18.5	2	0.	24	1.
Total identified to family	272	98.9	16,197	99.3	1,028	93.1	2,899	96.9	2,140	51.1

Fig. d. Distribution of the major fish groups found in the Later and Earlier phases of Trench J19 at Al Markh compared with those found in the Temple Saar, in Qala'at al-Bahrain and Shimal. The figures are the numbers of identified bones and the percentage of all bones identified to Doromosidae bones are vertebrae and have not been identified at sites other than Al Markh.

A summary chart records the main groups of fish identified from trench J19 (Fig. d left hand columns). In the upper layers fish-bone was much less well-preserved and there was much less of it, only 272 bones were identified. The results can be summarised as follows: in the upper layers and in the lower layers, particularly common species of fish were the sparidae or sea bream, and in the lower layers in particular this formed more than 80% of the identified fish-bone. In the upper layers the serranidae or groupers are more common, although the sparidae occur as a high proportion. The sparidae do not live at great depth, and are bottom feeders on sandy shores. It is interesting to compare the proportions of the fish-bones found in Al Markh with those found on other sites, for example at Saar, Qalat al Bahrain, or at the Bronze Age site of Shimal, in the United Arab Emirates (Fig. d right hand columns). Here the proportions are very different. The sparidae form a sizeable percentage of the fish-bone at these other sites but it seems that overall their fishing activities are quite different.

The reason for this probably is that Al Markh, at least in its early phase, seems to have been a very specialised fishing centre which was exploiting the spawning ground of the sea bream in the summer months between April and July, and that is why such a high proportion of the fish-bone belong to this family. It seems that at Shimal in particular they were exploiting a wider range of fish, not just the inland coastal fish, but also fish living further out at sea. At Saar and Qalat Al Bahrain there is evidence for fish living on rocky bottoms and coral reefs which are not present at Al Markh.

Analysis of the fish otoliths (the bones in the ears of fish which enable them to balance) is very informative. Because otoliths are very dense bones they are normally extremely well preserved, and on sites where no other bone is preserved if you sieve the sand you will often find them. Like shells and trees, they have growth rings: these are the result of monthly changes with the tides, each line representing the growth within a single month. Wim van Neer of the Netherlands has made thin sections of some 32 of these otoliths from Al Markh and in all but three of them the final rings are densely packed together which suggests that this represents growth in the early summer months. This finding in turn indicates that Al Markh may have been a seasonally occupied site specifically for the exploitation of sea bream.

Otoliths of other types of fish were also found in Al Markh including four of the giant salmon catfish. This is a particularly ugly fish of which apart from the otoliths only one skull fragment was identified at Al Markh. It is a fish that is seldom eaten in the region today, although it is very tasty, perhaps because it looks so unpleasant. One of the few small finds from Al Markh was a bead made out of an otolith from one of these fish.

In fact, there were very few small finds from Al Markh. There were three beads: the one made from an otolith, one from a dentalium or tusk shell, and one made from the hinge-shell of a spondylus or thorny oyster shell, all of which came from the later phase. From the later phase, too, came a bone point, while another came from the earlier phase together with a second bone artefact. These bone objects are probably made from sheep or goat bones.

The animal bone was first examined by Sebastian Payne and part of it later by Angela von den Driesch. In the later phase mammal bone was relatively abundant and equal in volume to the fish-bone. In this mammal bone collection were domesticated sheep or goat, which, when they could be identified as sheep or goat, were invariably goat. In the later phase, too, there are remains of the small Bahrain hare, which might have been exploited by the inhabitants of Al Markh or might have lived on the site after it had been abandoned.

There was an equid tooth, probably belonging to a donkey. Whether it was wild or domesticated could not be determined, but this would be rather early for domesticated donkey. On the other hand, it would be surprising if herds of wild donkeys were living on the relatively small island of Bahrain. There were also a few fragments of cattle bone, presumably domesticated. In the earlier layers there were three sheep/goat teeth which might have been contemporary, or which might have drifted in through animal holes or something like that. There were about a dozen fragments of dugong bones in these layers and one bone identified as belonging to an oryx. How this bone arrived in Bahrain is uncertain, but it could have been brought from the mainland.

After the animal bones the most frequent finds were shells and flint or chert fragments. From trench J19 came more than 7000 shells were collected, counted either by the spire for gastropods or by the hinge fragments for bivalves. These were, like the fish and mammal bone, unequally distributed, with the bulk of the shells belonging in the later layers rather than in the earlier ones. This is particularly the case with the smallest of the shells, the cerith-type or mitre shells, which were not exploited intentionally by the inhabitants of Al Markh but only arrived there as part of the beach-sand. In the later layers, the frequency of these shells is between 100 and 400 per cubic metre, whereas in the lower layers the frequency has dropped quite considerably, which is perhaps the result of the later layers being not in-situ but drifted in and mixed with the beach deposits in the area. The pearl oyster was the most commonly exploited shell in both the upper and the lower layers, and seems to have been collected for food, rather than for the pearls or for the mother-of-pearl which they produce. Fig. e gives an idea of contribution that each type of shell would have made to the diet. Here I calculate that about two thirds of the food contribution both in the later and in the earlier phase came from the pearl oyster. In the later phase murex snails provided about a quarter of the food contribution, while in the earlier phase Venus clams were more important. The distribution of these shells through the different layers was not uniform. In the lower layers the Venus clams were almost entirely in the midden with the fish-bones, whereas the sandy layers and the lower dark layers contained many fewer. This again suggests that the lower sandy layers just drifted in rather than being in-situ remains.

There was great deal of flint found at Al Markh which has been studied by Frances Healy. Like the other finds it was unevenly distributed. From the surface came three arrow-heads, and from the upper layers in J19 an arrow-head made out of tile flint, probably locally acquired (Fig. f bottom right). Of the tools, the most common tools were scrapers or knives, with the occasional borer or awl or chopper. There were about 64 cores and 150 tools (over 80% of them in the later layers) out of a total of more than 6000 pieces of flint. There were about 150 intact flakes, but the bulk of the flint (almost 95%) consisted of irregular fragments or broken flakes. The great majority of the flint (about 90%), both by number of pieces and by weight, was in the later phase, whereas in the earlier phase the amount of flint was relatively small (Fig.c).

The final category of finds that I want to discuss is perhaps not statistically so significant comprising only 151 pieces, compared with the hundreds of thousands of fish-bones and thousands of shells and pieces of flint, but it is one that is of interest, namely the pottery sherds which gave rise to the original interest in the site. The distribution of these, too, is very uneven. There were eight in the later layers, and 143 in the earlier layers, and it seems very probable that the eight in the later layers were not in-situ but are earlier material that has been incorporated in the later sand. It seems probable that at Al Markh we have an unusual sequence going from a ceramic-using culture to a culture which is aceramic with no pottery.

The pottery is of a mainly pale green, rather hard-fired ware, with rather simple decoration on it in bands, (Fig. g) and this has been identified as Late Ubaid, or even post-Ubaid pottery dating to the late fifth millennium BC in Mesopotamia. A similar sherd was found on the surface at Al Markh, another came from the neighbouring site (2070) where I mentioned the flint was found, and a sherd possibly of Ubaid date was found at the site of Diraz East. Several of the sherds from Al

Type of shell	relative size	Later phase			Earlier phase		
		number	amount of food	%	number	amount of food	%
Pearl oyster	50	732	18,300	66.7	515	12,875	64.6
Small trochid snail	4	73	268	1.1	164	648	3.3
Small murex snail	8	159	1,272	4.6	51	408	2.1
Venus clam	64	1	32	0.1	150	4,800	24.1
Large murex snail	64	114	7,296	26.6	10	640	3.2
Limpet	10	13	130	0.5	12	120	0.6
Small trochid snail	2	12	24	0.1	8	16	0.1
Tiny periwinkle	1	0	0	0.0	11	11	0.1
Cockle	64	0	0	0.0	10	320	1.6
Lucine	40	5	100	0.4	4	80	0.4
totals		1,109	27,422		935	19,918	

Fig. e. The numbers and approximate food contribution in arbitrary units (tiny periwinkle = 1) of the most common edible shells from the Later and Earlier phases in Trench J19.

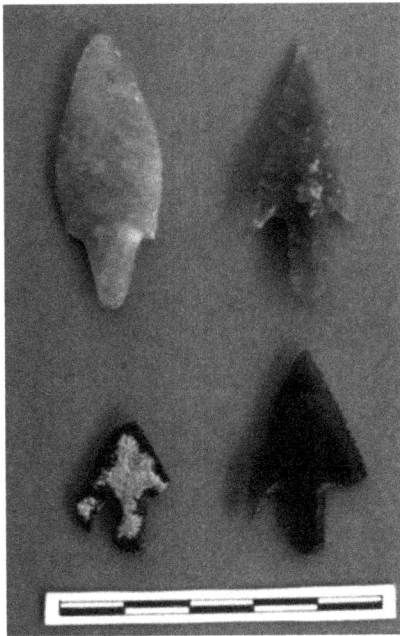

Fig. f. Bi-facial Arrowheads

Fig.g. Ubaid painted pottery

Markh showed signs of having been drilled, which is normally interpreted as showing that the pots were cracked or broken and then mended with string or twine pulling the joins together. This suggests that pottery was not readily available. Other sherds show evidence of the edges being filed down, which may again mean that when the rim of a pot broke, rather than acquiring a new pot, they just smoothed the edge and continued using the lower part of the vessel. It would seem that the people did not have ready access to pottery.

In the late 1970s Joan Oates and Hugh Mackerrell (Oates at al 1977) published a study of the Ubaid period pottery found in eastern Arabia, Bahrain, Qatar, and through neutron activation analysis they identified the proportions of various chemical elements and used them as a finger-print to identify the source of the clay out of which the pots were made. They compared these results with pottery from three sites in southern Mesopotamia (Uruk, Ubaid and Eridu) and came to the conclusion that the majority of the Ubaid style pottery in the Gulf actually came from the site of Ur itself. Subsequently my sister, Jane Galbraith, who is a statistician, re-analysed the data (Roaf & Galbraith 1994) and discovered that their assumptions were wrong, and that although they thought that they had proved that the pottery, with a high degree of probability, actually came from the site of Ur, the results actually showed is that it is possible that it came from Ur, but it might well have come from other sites in south Mesopotamia. Furthermore 10% of the clay of the analysed sherds from the Gulf is not compatible with a south Mesopotamian origin and probably came from elsewhere, but where exactly is not known. There is also some red pottery with a totally different finger-print to the Mesopotamian pottery, that may have been produced locally or have come from some third place. About two weeks before the seminar I got the results of some thin-section petrographic analysis of pottery from Al Markh, carried out by Robert Mason of the Royal Ontario Museum in Toronto, and in this he confirmed that the trends shown by the neutron activation analysis were similar to those in thin-sections. Of the seven sherds that he analysed, five of them had mineral inclusions which are very similar to the sort of mineral inclusion you find in southern Mesopotamian clays. One of them is similar to the type of clay used in later periods in Bahrain, in the Barbar culture, and he suggests that this is of local origin. The final sherd is rather unusual with some rather interesting inclusions which are closest in character to clays that are now found in Oman. This is quite surprising. We know now that there are sites in the United Arab Emirates that have Ubaid style pottery, but up until now there is no evidence that Oman had contact with the Ubaid culture or that there was any pottery being made in Oman. I think it is probably a bit too early to draw the conclusion that pottery was actually being imported from Oman. I think we may find another source of similar clays closer to Bahrain, perhaps in Iran or elsewhere, from which this sherd could have come.

To conclude, the site of Al Markh has produced interesting results. It seems to be a very unusual, or untypical, site compared to other sites investigated in the region. Its earlier phase (probably to be dated towards the end of the fifth millennium BC) relied to a great extent on the fishing of one group of fish, the sparidae. How this was done is not clear. They may have used fish traps like modern Bahraini fishermen. The location of Al Markh on an island off the coast of Bahrain would have been well suited for such a fishing method. They might have erected a barrier between the island and the mainland and the fish would have been swept in by the tides and then trapped. On the other hand, they may have used nets and some of the larger fish may have been caught at sea from boats. In the later phase (perhaps to be dated in the fourth millennium BC) there was a different economy, still relying to a great extent on marine resources but also with the addition of sheep/goat husbandry to add to their resources.

Acknowledgements

I would like to express my thanks to the Bahrain Department of Antiquities, to the sponsors of the expedition, to the team members, and to the specialists who have helped with the analysis of the finds. In preparing my talk for this publication I am very grateful to Harriet Crawford for her efforts.

LIVING AT SAAR:
DILMUN AT THE START OF THE SECOND MILLENNIUM BC

Robert KILLICK

1. INTRODUCTION

Sometime during the last quarter of the third millennium BC something odd happened in Bahrain: people decided to build permanent settlements out of stone. This is not to say that there were no earlier towns and villages but that, if there were, then they were built of flimsier material than limestone and have left no trace in the archaeological record. While this was an innovation for Bahrain, it was not so for the Arabian Gulf as a whole where an earlier tradition of building in stone is found in the Emirates (Frifelt 1995)

Whatever the impetus behind this change, it marks in the archaeological record Bahrain's rise to prominence as *the* major maritime power in the area. By the end of the third millennium and through the first quarter of the second, the Dilmun civilisation, based in Bahrain, dominated the northern half of the Gulf.

In Bahrain itself, this period of prosperity is characterised by a construction boom (plus ça change…). Thus we see the expansion of the main city at Qala'at al-Bahrain and the construction of the town wall and warehouses, new temples at Barbar, Diraz and Saar, an extensive redevelopment of the Saar settlement, and the first appearance of the vast burial fields which, until recently, dominated the landscape of Bahrain. Taken together, these developments indicate the emergence of (or increased power of) a centralised Dilmun state, headed by a king (Hojlund 1997: 41).

Inevitably, bust followed boom. By the second quarter of the second millennium, Dilmun had lost its pre-eminence as a trading power and was in economic decline, the temples were no longer maintained and settlements had either contracted or been entirely abandoned.

These broader historical processes of growth and decline are reflected in the particular history of settlement at Saar. We can chart the progress of Saar from the early days, when it was just a few buildings clustered in the centre of the settlement, through a period of systematic redevelopment and rapid expansion, and on into one of retrenchment and abandonment.

2. THE DEVELOPMENT OF THE SAAR SETTLEMENT

Chronology

The basic chronological information from Saar comes from eight C14 determinations and from the relative dating of the pottery. Other parts of the assemblage, such as seals or chlorite bowls, do not provide significant additional chronological data. The C14 determinations, even at 90%+ confidence range, do no more than tell us that we are roughly in the right centuries. The Saar pottery can be tied to the sequence from Qala'at al-Bahrain and to the dates for the various periods of that site as proposed in the relevant publications. The data are summarised in Table 1.[1]

The stratigraphically oldest C14 determination from Saar 1 provides a range of 2670 – 2340 BC (94.1% confidence) for the start of the settlement. This date is at best 200 years earlier than the one suggested by pottery parallels (2100 – 2000 BC), but it should be noted that in the temple sounding Saar 1 was represented by 3m of deposit, a greater depth than all the succeeding levels put together. Though it is difficult to equate depth of deposit with the passing of years, this prompts the suggestion that Saar 1 might have spanned more than a century.

The major period of expansion at Saar (Saar 2 and 3) spans most or all of the 20th and 19th centuries BC.

A date for the end of the settlement is problematic: there are no C14 determinations from Saar 4, and very little pottery. The end of Saar 3 is put at around 1800 BC. Saar 4 is of short duration archaeologically and therefore could be contained within the first quarter of the 18th century BC.

---

[1] The archaeological sequence at Saar has been divided into four main levels based on the stratigraphic evidence alone and without reference to seriations of other components of the assemblage. These divisions have been labelled as Saar 1 – 4, from bottom to top. A study of the pottery has resulted in a three-fold division (Pottery Periods 1 – 3), from earlier to later, with the latter subdivided into 3a and 3b. These two sequences do not correspond exactly, nor would we expect them to.

Table 1: Chronological Data

SAAR LEVEL	Sample/Uncallibrated	Callibrated (95.4% probability)	Saar Pottery period	Qala'at al-Bahrain period	Qala'at al-Bahrain date[2]
SAAR 1	BM-2873 : 4000±50BP BM-2872 : 3740±40BP BM-2870 : 3700±80BP	2670BC (94.1%) 2340BC 2840BC (1.3%) 2810BC 2290BC (94.3%) 2020BC 2000BC (1.1%) 1980BC 2400BC (95.4%) 1800BC	1	2A early 2B	2050-1950BC
SAAR 2	OxA-5913 : 3320±130BP OxA-8275 : 3665±30BP	1950BC (95.4%) 1250BC 2140BC (95.4%) 1940BC	2	2B	1950-1900BC
SAAR 3	OxA-8276 : 3670±50BP OxA-8277 : 3595±45BP OxA-8278 : 3355±35BP	2150BC (89.6%) 1890BC 2200BC (5.8%) 2160BC 2050BC (81.5%) 1870BC 2130BC (4.7%) 2080BC 1850BC (9.2%) 1770BC 1740BC (95.4%) 1520BC	3A 3B	2C after 2C, before 2F	1900-1800 BC 1800BC-
SAAR 4	No data		3B?		

Saar 1: The Early Days

Little is known about the earliest period at Saar. It is clear that to begin with settlement was restricted to a core area in and around the central part of the site. Stone-built rectilinear buildings are found in this level, but the street pattern so characteristic of later levels has yet to emerge. Equally, there is no exact precursor to the temple that later came to dominate the settlement. We can speculate that by this time the large mound field that bordered the western edge of the settlement was in use. This subsequently spread out over most of the limestone ridge on which the settlement was built.

Life must have been quite pleasant during the early days of Saar. The settlement was in an elevated position, catching the breeze, and from their houses the inhabitants could look out eastwards on a broad band of palm trees and gardens, beyond which lay a coastal inlet where shellfish were collected and fish caught. Fish and dates were the staples of the Dilmun diet. Freshwater too was provided in abundance by springs fed from the aquifer which underlies the northern half of Bahrain.

The ease with which the essentials of life, particularly water, could be obtained in Dilmun stands in stark contrast to the enormous effort that was put into controlling through irrigation the potentially destructive waters of the Tigris and Euphrates Rivers in southern Babylonia. It is easy to see why the inhabitants of the latter place thought that life in Dilmun was akin to paradise.

But this original state of anarchy, if that is what it was, was not allowed to persist for long. As Dilmun trade prospered, along with it came standardisation (of weights and measures, for example), regulation, enforcement and bureaucracy...

Saar 2 and 3: The settlement in its Prime

The settlement at Saar was re-developed sometime in the 20th century BC. This event is characterized by the emergence of rectangular blocks[3] of buildings containing up to four or five separate units, the establishment of the main street and the construction of the temple (Saar 2).

Excavation to the foundation level of many of the blocks showed that they were constructed quite close together in time, with only 10 – 20 cm of sand separating neighbouring blocks. Although we do not know what time span is represented by these deposits. our interpretation is that it is short and indicates a period of rapid expansion.

About 80 buildings of Saar 2/3 have been excavated or identified. Adding in an estimate for those buildings that lie in unexcavated parts of the site, Saar in its prime contained about 130 buildings, spread over 2.5 hectares.

By and large, the Saar 2 blocks each underwent one major rebuild, as opposed to minor episodes of re-flooring or small architectural adjustments.

This is true not only of the buildings grouped around the temple, but even of those in the South-eastern Quarter. These

---

[2] Dates for Qala'at al-Bahrain taken from Fig. 29 (p26) of Hojlund 1997.

[3] Our definition of a "block" as used here is a row or group of buildings with shared walls that is either separated from its neighbours on all sides by open spaces (i.e. streets or squares) or on a different orientation. Most blocks at Saar conform to this definition, but sometimes the definition is applied a little more arbitrarily.

rebuilds have been assigned to Saar 3. The nature and extent of the Saar 3 rebuilds vary from block to block. Generally, they respect the earlier house and block boundaries. Some buildings however, were not rebuilt but left abandoned (Bldgs 62, 226 and 300 for example), and elsewhere new buildings with a different plan appear (such as Bldg 56). It is a natural consequence of the way buildings were constructed in rows with shared walls that major rebuilds had to be done across a block at the same time, and although the rebuilds to different blocks did not start from exactly the same archaeological horizon, the difference is generally of the same order of magnitude as noted above for the Level 1 horizons. It is, however, an oversimplification to place all these rebuilds into Level 3 and, by doing so, we are disguising what was a more complicated process of redevelopment that was both on-going and piecemeal.

Saar 4: In Decline

The ensuing period at Saar (Saar 4) is one of contraction, with only a few new buildings dated to this level. These include an industrial kiln (Bldg 36), Bldg 50 in the Central Quarter and Bldg 9 on the opposite side of Janabiyah Street. These three buildings all intrude into the previously established street pattern, indicating a breakdown for whatever reason of the regulatory mechanisms visible in previous levels. The construction of a large gypsum kiln in the middle of a residential area of the settlement was accompanied by the abandonment of many of the surrounding buildings. Many other buildings in the settlement were also falling into disrepair at this time and show evidence of intermittent use only.

The decline and then abandonment of the settlement cannot be explained by reference to the archaeological evidence from Saar which tells us *what* happened but not *why*. The settlement was in a favourable position and provided with a good supply of the necessities of life (food and water) so on the face of it there seems no reason why people should not have gone on living at Saar indefinitely.

However, the abandonment of Saar was not an isolated occurrence: all other known settlements on Bahrain fell into ruin at the same time. The usual reasons given for this event relate to changing patterns of international trade, in particular the decline of Ur and of the cities of the Indus, Dilmun's main trading partners (Crawford 2000: 76). It seems unlikely, however, that this led to a *total* retreat from permanent settlement on Bahrain itself, given the favourable living conditions.

3. LAYOUT AND ORGANIZATION

The settlement at Saar hugs the edge of the limestone outcrop that looks out over the northern plain of Bahrain. It is about 2.5 hectares in extent. The major characteristic of the settlement is the rectangular blocks of buildings that contain two, three or four separate units. These blocks naturally produce a grid-like system of streets and squares, of which the most prominent is the broad main artery. This street (Main Street) has been traced over a distance of 230 m. In places it is as much as 7.5 m wide, though north of the temple its character changes and it narrows to only 4 m. Side roads branch off and lead into small public squares. The most prominent building is the temple which stands at the junction of Main Street with another road that comes in from the east. The appearance of order and regularity in the settlement layout overall is reflected in the conformity of individual buildings which show little variety of design.

Standard buildings

The most common (and simplest) building at Saar is, in effect, a rectangular room which is partitioned off in one corner to create a second, inner room.[4] This inner room is located on the front wall of the building next to the entrance from the street or square. The outer room has two distinct areas. Next to the main door its width is constrained by the walls of the inner room so that a passageway is created. At the rear of the building the passageway opens into the main part of the outer room which runs across the full width of the building. There is a second entrance on the rear wall immediately opposite the one on the front wall. The door into the inner room is always on the wall facing away from the front entrance. In most, the inner room is located on the left hand-side when entering a building from the street or square. Constructing the inner room always on the same side ensures that the inner rooms of adjacent buildings are never contiguous.

Excluding partially excavated buildings and those where there are uncertainties about some aspects of the plan, there are 28 examples of this building type.[5] These have been labelled our A-Series buildings. Our next commonest building type (D-Series) has an additional enclosed area at the rear of the building, but is otherwise identical.[6] There are fourteen examples of this type.

Not only do all these buildings have identical plans, but they contain the same range of domestic installations: ovens, hearths, pits and basins, usually found in identical positions within the building.

If we look at the relative frequency of the various sorts of installations in the building (Table 2), then the commonest ones are a stone-built jar support with trough (Type 400), a plastered pit (Type 300), a *tannur* (Type 200), a coned jar support (Types 210/211) and a hearth (Types 201/202). We could reasonably expect a standard building to contain most, if not all, of these features.

---

[4] Previous publications on Saar have referred to these buildings as "L-shaped" houses or "houses with "L-shaped rooms". In retrospect, I do not think either is a particularly useful or accurate term.

[5] This and other figures relating to building types should be considered provisional, as the analysis is still continuing at the time of writing.

[6] The B- and C-Series contain buildings where the two rooms are arranged differently.

Table 2: Distribution of Common Installation types in A- and D- Series Buildings

Bldg Series / Installation codes		105	200	201	202	203	204	205	210	211	300	310	311	400	Total
Builidng 2	A1														0
52	A1										x				1
55	A1			x						x	x			x	4
57	A1			x						x			x		3
63	A1			x				x						x	3
64	A1	x	x		x		x			x	x				5
100	A1	x	x			x					x			x	4
104	A1	x					x				x			x	3
206	A1														0
207	A1	x	x	x					x		x			x	5
220	A1	x	x		x		x	x	x		x			x	7
221	A1		x											x	2
223	A1										x			x	2
226	A1	x	x		x				x					x	4
102	A1.2		x											x	2
225	A2	x	x				x	x			x		x		6
1	A3		x								x			x	3
208	D1	x	x	x		x	x	x	x		x				7
209	D1	x	x	x			x	x	x	x	x			x	8
211	D1		x				x		x	x		x		x	6
224	D1		x		x						x		x	x	5
3	D2						x				x		x		3
4	D2		x				x			x	x				4
9	D2						x	x							2
204	D2	x	x			x	x		x		x		x	x	7
205	D2	x		x			x			x	x			x	5
300	D2		x	x			x		x					x	5
202	D3										x	x			2
203	D4	x	x	x			x		x	x	x			x	7
301	D5		x								x			x	3
302	D6	x	x	x							x			x	5
Present in: Out of 31		13	19	10	4	3	14	5	9	13	20	1	5	20	

The first of these, a stone-built jar support with a plastered trough, was used for water storage/washing. It is usually found just inside the main door of the outer room. Out of 53 examples in all types of buildings, only 7 were located elsewhere. The jar support is built of solid stone with the sides faced with plaster. The top is not often intact, but one example had a stone edging around a central depression The trough is set a few centimetres lower than the bench and finished with a coat of hard white plaster, with the bottom sloping down towards the front of the installation. In some cases, a drainage lip was still preserved. Instead of a plastered trough, two examples have half of a jar set into the stone surround, presumably serving a similar function.

Tannurs, a particular and distinctive type of oven, were also located most commonly in the outer room. Each *tannur* has a circular stone superstructure built around the cooking chamber which is made from a single pottery sleeve inserted into the stonework. They are heavily plastered, with a finishing coat of smooth white plaster over an ashy bedding layer.

Coned jar supports are also found overwhelmingly in the outer room. They consist of two or more upright plastered stones, usually set along the wall next to a semicircular hearth, and so spaced that a round-bottomed cooking pot can be supported between them.

It is quite clear from the above that the outer room was the favoured location for many of these installations and therefore where most activity took place. By contrast the inner rooms are usually devoid of them. The rear rooms of D-Series buildings are also relatively empty of installations, though some do contain concentrations of plastered pits. A detailed analysis of the distribution and frequency of pottery types has suggested that these rear rooms were used for the storage of large jars and their contents and possibly for brewing (Carter forthcoming). There is also a correlation between serving vessels and the outer rooms of buildings, while the pottery from the inner rooms suggests they were used for more general storage purposes.

Buildings that have a similar plan and contain a standard set of installations are interpreted as having an identical function. In the case of Saar, the A- and D- Series buildings share the attributes of domestic buildings. If we can make another assumption, namely that buildings of a different plan but with the same range of installations (and finds) also served an identical purpose, then nearly all the buildings at Saar can be considered as work-a-day houses.

This is not to say that some did not serve additional purposes as well, or had more room to carry out the same range of activities, both of which have implications for social diversity.

Non-standard Buildings

There are some odd grouping of rooms and areas where the inter-relationships are unclear. These are still being analysed. Currently, however, there is only one rectilinear building that is clearly different from the standard types: Bldg 56 which lies on the east side of Main Street. The rooms of this building were arranged in an odd pattern and some were heavily coated with a hard gypsum plaster. Entrance was from Main Street through a larger opening than normal (1.20 m compared with 60 - 80 cm). Immediately on the left was a small, heavily plastered room. A room at the rear was entirely taken up by a large plastered tank, while a second tank lay outside the back-door of the building. The largest room contained a distinctly odd installation, comprising a bench with plastered grooves. None of the standard installation types were present. The combination of an unusual plan, the treatment of the rooms, and the absence of standard installations indicate a special function for this building. Although we do not know specifically what this was, it included the storage of liquids (or materials) that required a waterproof lining and presumably some processing.

A second structure which is clearly different is a free-standing, oval-shaped building intruding into Janabiyah Square (Bldg 36). It measured 3.10 x 5.30 m. across, with walls standing 50 cm high. The top courses of stonework inclined inward suggesting a conical or domed superstructure. Inside there was a long narrow firepit dug into the floor and large deposits of burnt material which contained small pieces of a soft white stone. Analysis has demonstrated that this material was gypsum and that the building was a kiln for producing gypsum plaster.[7]

The Temple

No account of the Saar settlement would be complete without a mention of the temple[8]. It was the largest and most important building and occupied a central spot in the settlement, at the crossroads of the major arteries. It had a long life and was extensively renovated, outlasting most of the neighbouring buildings. Though we have no idea about the exact nature or extent of its influence it must have played an important role in the life of the inhabitants. The location of the temple (and indeed of the settlement) so close to one of the major Dilmun burial fields is suggestive of cause and effect, though in what order remains unknown.

4. FUNCTION OF THE SETTLEMENT

The inhabitants of Saar, in their smart new houses, do not seem to have had any unusual pastimes. We assume that they were actually engaged in producing the range of foodstuffs for which we have evidence (i.e. fishing, date cultivation, and animal husbandry) and most households seem to have needed a seal, and so were engaged in at least a minimal level of economic activity (Crawford 2001: 45). The range of imported goods indicates wider horizons, though most foreign goods might have been obtained from Qala'at al-Bahrain rather than from further afield. The list includes soft stone, igneous stones, carnelian, copper, ivory and bitumen. The importation of bitumen is a curiosity as analysis has shown that the Saar inhabitants used bitumen from Iran whereas at Qala-at al-Bahrain it came from Iraq (Conan et al 1999). Why two settlements so close together should get the same commodity from two different sources is not clear, but it does suggest that Saar still retained some autonomy in matters of trade and commerce.

The general uniformity of architecture through Levels 2 and 3 is the most striking characteristic of the Saar settlement, but its interpretation is difficult. This is because the archaeological evidence from Saar does not cast any light on why the settlement was built in this fashion. Our immediate assumption on looking at the plan is that it is so orderly and repetitive that someone must have been controlling the process. If we accept this gloss on the architecture, namely that order – in this case, architectural order – is a sign of authority, then it becomes relatively easy to suggest which authority was responsible. Other straws in the wind indicate that Dilmun by this time had an administrative elite perhaps headed by a king living at Qala'at al-Bahrain, a city which was by now a fortified settlement of considerable size containing monumental storerooms (Hojlund 1989: 54 & 2000: 61). Saar lies only 7 km away from Qala'at al-Bahrain – one hour's comfortable walking – and so would have fallen easily into the administrative orbit of such a king and his officials.

The standardised building plans might also suggest that the settlement was built for a specialised purpose. The repetition of form clearly indicates a repetition of function, as do the standardised installations and, to some extent, the sameness of the finds assemblage. But this only allows us to say that most inhabitants were engaged in roughly the same range of activities – something which is true of most ancient settlements of similar size to Saar. It may be that some very specific purpose, such as living-quarters for workmen, lay behind the standard building plans at Saar, but the case for this rests solely on the interpretation of the regularity of the architecture.

Since Saar is the only settlement of Early Dilmun date that has been excavated, it is simply unclear if its standard

---

[7] This analysis was kindly undertaken by Dr. G.C. Morgan, School of Archaeological Studies, University of Leicester.

[8] For a detailed account of this building, see Crawford, Killick & Moon (eds) 1997).

architecture is either unique or typical of the Early Dilmun period. What can be noted is that rectilinear stone buildings have been found at both Diraz[9] and at al-Hajjar[10] and, at the former, there were also domestic installations similar to the Saar examples. This might suggest that Saar is not an atypical example.

5. CONCLUSION

The people who were living at Saar at the start of the second millennium BC were part of a stable and increasingly populous and prosperous community. Stability in the Gulf region was a prerequisite for the smooth running of the Dilmun trading networks. Domestically at Saar, the archaeological record reveals an orderliness and continuity which lasted as long as two hundred years. The expansion that accompanied Saar Period 2 shows that the population was increasing, while the presence of a range of imported goods and of seals and sealings reflects the commercial confidence of the time. The inhabitants of Saar may not have been major-league businessmen, but at the very least they enjoyed some of the "trickle-down" benefits of the new economic cycle.

When the economic downturn came, the response of those living at Saar was to depart, not necessarily suddenly or all at once, but perhaps over one or two generations. This mirrors events elsewhere in Dilmun. Subsequent settlements in Bahrain as a whole, over the following two thousand years plus that preceded Islam, are elusive in the archaeological record. We may speculate that one reason for this is that for much of the time the inhabitants of Bahrain may have lived in houses built from materials less durable than stone, perhaps palm-frond *barastis*. This speculation is equally valid for pre-Dilmun times. In which case, Early Dilmun settlements such as Saar, with stone-built houses, may best be viewed as temporary and alien intrusions in a landscape that otherwise remained more or less unchanged up until the modern era.

References

Al-Tikriti, Abdul Kader 1975. Diraz excavation and its chronological position. *Dilmun* 8: 16-20

Carter, R. forthcoming. The Pottery of Saar. In Killick R and Moon J (eds) *The Dilmun Settlement at Saar*.

Crawford H, 2001. *Early Dilmun Seals from Saar*.

Crawford, HEW 2000. Bahrain: Warehouse of the Gulf. *Traces of Paradise* 72-76.

Crawford H, Killick R & Moon J (eds) 1997. *The Dilmun temple at Saar*.

Frifelt 1995: *The Island of Umm an-Nar Vol 2 The Third Millennium Settlement*. JASP XXVI: 2.

Hojlund F, 1989. The Formation of the Dilmun State and the Amorite Tribes. *PSAS* 19: 45-59.

Hojlund F, 1997. *Qala'at al-Bahrain 2 The Central Monumental Buildings*. JASPXXX: 2.

Hojlund F, 2000. Qala'at al-Bahrain in the Bronze Age. *Traces of Paradise*. 59-62.

---

[9] See al-Tikriti 1975. The settlement around the Diraz Temple was subsequently destroyed by development in the mid-90s, but not before one building had been excavated by the Department of Antiquities.

[10] Rectilinear buildings were found at al-Hajjar in the course of excavating Early Dilmun burial mounds. The settlement lay only 300 m southwest of the al-Hajjar grave complex with which it was presumably associated. The material remains unpublished.

Figure 1 Schematic plan of Saar

Figure 2 The settlement and plain from the air

Figure 3 A row of identical buildings

Figure 4 A Standard A-Series Building (Bldg 226)

Figure 5 Standard installations (a) Jar support with plastered trough (b) Coned jar support (c) Tannur

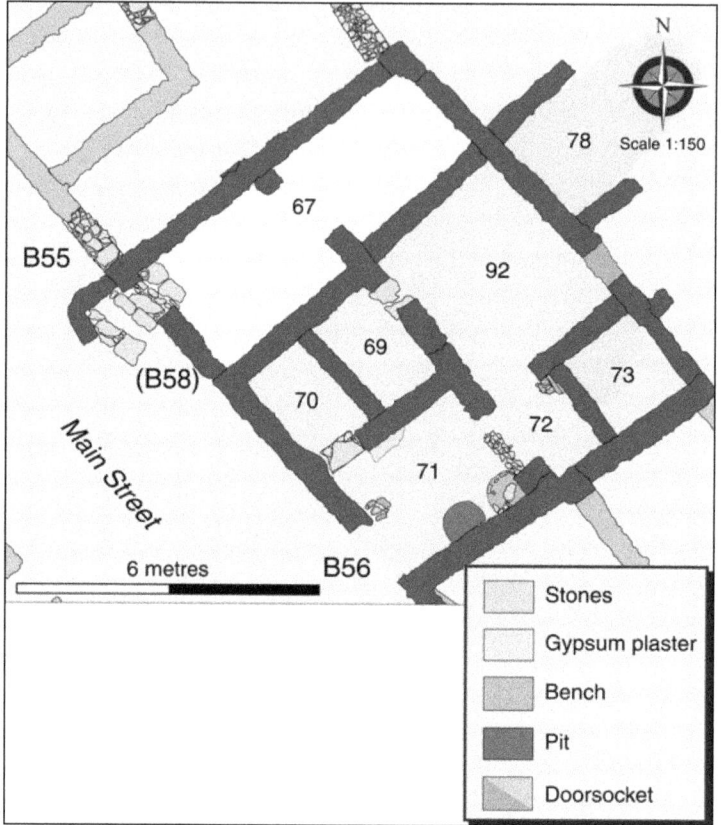

Figure 6 Plan of Bldg 56

Figure 7 Plastered rooms in Bldg 56

Figure 8 Gypsum kiln

Figure 9 The Temple from the air

Figure 10 Bitumen beads

EXCAVATIONS AT DIRAZ EAST AND A'ALI EAST

Michael ROAF

The second site investigated by the British Archaeological Expedition to Bahrain was that of Diraz East.(Map) The major occupation of the site dates to the early second millennium during the Early Dilmun or Barbar period when many of the very extensive tumulus burial fields were constructed covering large areas of nortern Bahrain (estimated as more than 25 square kilometres in extent). The burial mounds were normally situated on land above the level of the springs, which was therefore unsuitable for irrigation and cultivation. The most impressive of these monuments are the so-called royal burials of A'ali, many of which were originally more than 20 m high. Some were later used as kilns and, although robbed in antiquity, they are still imposing.

There are several other significant sites in Bahrain dating to the Early Dilmun period including Qala'at al-Bahrain, Barbar and Saar. The Dilmun Period is conventionally divided into an Early Dilmun phase which lasted roughly from the last quarter of the third millennium to about 1600 BC, a Middle Dilmun phase roughly contemporary with the Middle Babylonian Period in Mesopotamia (about 1600-1000 BC), and a Late Dilmun phase, which lasted from about 1000 BC to the end of the Achaemenid period in about 300BC. This paper deals mostly with remains of the Early Dilmun period, but because we excavated a tomb from the Late Dilmun period at Diraz East and two more of the same date at A'ali East, some information about them will also be given. Space and time does not allow me to discuss the remains of later periods excavated in A'ali East

The Early Dilmun period was a time of extensive settlement and remarkable prosperity on the island of Bahrain. Archaeologically it is most recognisable by the rather ugly pottery known as Barbar pottery (named after the site of Barbar excavated by the Danish mission), which has exploded yellow 'measles' in the clay left by burnt out calcareous inclusions. The agricultural wealth of Bahrain based on its abundant fresh water springs was certainly an important factor in the development of the Early Dilmun culture. Another reason for its prosperity is that Bahrain, which was an important part of the country of Dilmun, lay on the trade route between the Harappan civilisation and the Mesopotamia civilisation. We know from cuneiform texts found in southern Mesopotamian cities that there was an important trade in copper brought from Oman, known at that time as Magan, in which the traders of Dilmun played a significant part. Very little about this trade is known from archaeological sources: some stamp seals similar to those used in Bahrain in the Early Dilmun period have been found in Mesopotamia and one in the Harappan port city of Lothal, Indus Valley style etched carnelian beads have been identified in Mesopotamian sites (Potts 1990 esp. chaps 5/6), and a few objects inscribed in Indus script have been excavated in Oman, Bahrain and Mesopotamia. Furthermore stone weights of both Mesopotamian and Harappan types were in use in Bahrain. In general, however, the archaeological record is scanty and it is only from the cuneiform texts that we know about the valuable cargoes of copper, timber, and of precious stones which were imported by the Dilmun traders. Among the precious stones are some called in Sumerian 'stone fish-eyes' and, although it has been suggested that this might be a type of agate, it seems more likely that they were pearls, which were one of the main exports from Bahrain in later periods, since in fact they look very similar to boiled fish-eyes.

The site of Diraz East lies in the north-west of the island beside the road from Manama to Budaiya in an area of Bahrain which is now very heavily built-up and which in the 1970s was under threat. Tony McNicoll started the excavations there in 1973/4 and found some plastered stone pillars and a podium, and then had to stop the excavation. The following year it was not possible to work there and we resumed in 1976 for a month, and completed the excavation and conservation of the site in a two month season in 1977/8. The area of Diraz is full of ancient monuments, including the wells of Umm al-Sejour and a site excavated by Abdul Qader al-Tikriti (al-Tikriti 1975), but now most of the ancient remains in the Diraz area have either been destroyed or lie buried under housing and development. The area available for our excavations in Diraz, lay just to the north north of the Budaiya highway (Map). Great channels had been dug to the north and east by developers to get sand for their building operations and large numbers of stamp seals were apparently found in these excavations, some of which have made their way into various museums and private collections.

The remains of the Early Dilmun buildings at Diraz East were close to the surface with the result that the floors of the building were very fragmentary. We found areas of harder sand which we followed for a few feet and then they would fade away. We could seldom identify definite floors although it was clear from the evidence of the plaster on the columns there had originally been floors at several different levels. The sections were also remarkably uninformative. An Australian member of our team said it was like digging inside an egg-timer, with the sand just dripping off the walls down into the trenches. There were also many later pits of various periods and other disturbances.

Very few objects were found in the buildings and the pottery that was recovered, mostly sherds of Barbar ware, was not in situ. Where we found floor levels in the temple they were

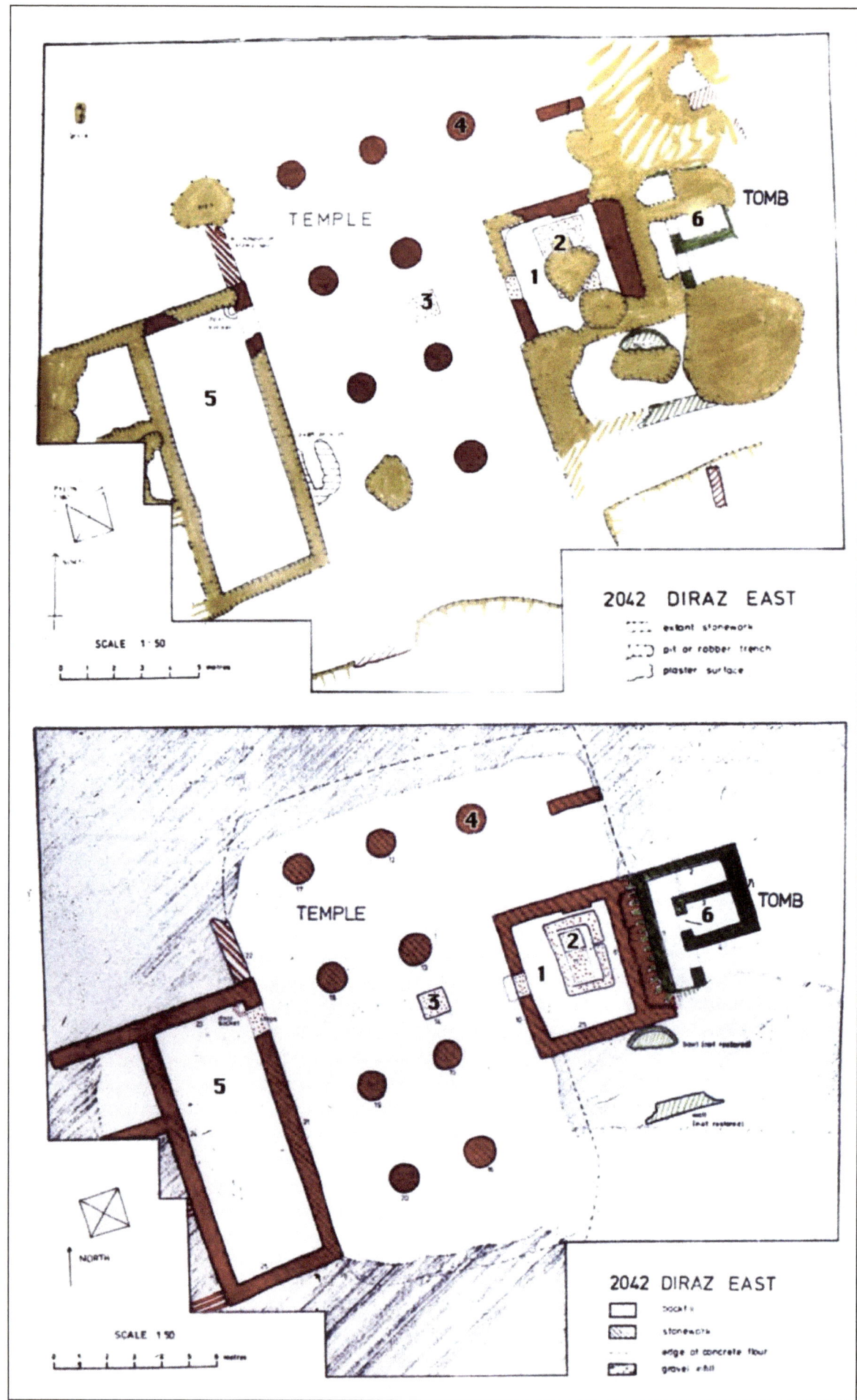

Plate: Plans of the excavations at Diraz East before (a) and after (b) the reconstruction.

invariably very clean without pottery on them. In spite of this, there is no doubt that the building that we found does belong to the Early Dilmun period (probably to the later part of it according to the typology of the sherds). The plan (Plate) shows the structures that were standing above ground belonging to the temple, some later structures, and pits and robber trenches. It was quite difficult in some cases to identify these pits because pits dug into sand and filled with sand are almost impossible to excavate.

The main features of the temple are reasonably clear. In a rectangular room [1] there was an altar or podium [2]. In front of this room there was a another rectangular podium [3] and then two rows of circular structures [4] which we called columns, although their original height is impossible to determine. The altar [2] would have been the most interesting feature of the site had not a 16/17th century pit removed part of it. It is clear that it had a plastered surround with a channel and from traces of the foundations it clearly extended over the area of this large pit. There might have been two platforms originally, or less likely, a long, continuous, platform. The back wall seemed to have only one face and to have been dug into the earlier deposits with its west face being covered with gypsum plaster. The other walls were made out of stone and plastered with gypsum. In places the gypsum plaster survived higher than the stonework. This is because the stones were robbed out at a later date for re-use in a new building leaving the plaster face intact. West of Room 1 were the foundations for a stone structure, perhaps the foundation for a wall, which may not have gone up to ceiling height. In the middle of it were a couple of flat stones, on which there was an outline of some circular object, perhaps an altar. It originally stood in the middle of the entrance but was later removed. In front of that was a square pillar, slightly tapering, which was raised in height at a later date when more stones were added.

Beyond that stood the rows of columns, one of which was completely robbed out by a pit, dug presumably to remove the stones. A fragment of walling was found north of Room 1 and possibly there would have been a corresponding wall to the south as well an additional column. West of this surviving row of circular structures there were some additional rooms [5] but beyond that the slope of the ground means that all remains have been destroyed. The ground level drops all round the building. It is possible that there was originally a revetment wall and that the building stood on some sort of a platform but it was not well enough preserved to be able to determine that with certainty. Room 5 had a door socket in the corner, and here we found a rather nice Early Dilmun stamp seal with a dragon-like monster on it (Fig. a) Stone-robbers removed most of the walls of this room leaving behind only trenches dug into the sand and filled with sand.

In the final season we had to decide what we should do with the site after we had excavated it. One possibility was to back-fill it, but that might have allowed someone to build on the site and so we decided to restore the site as far as we could, in order to preserve it. This involved rebuilding the missing elements. We filled in the pits and rebuilt the walls

Fig. a. Stamp seal of Early Dilmun type from Room 5 at Diraz East

of Room 1 and the altar. We also rebuilt the missing walls and column. On top of the walls and columns we built an extra two courses of stone work to protect them and we laid a new floor with gypsum mortar. We back-filled the surrounding area with sand so that it came over the edge of the floor. The reconstructd temple has survived reasonably well and forms a valuable addition to Bahrain's archaeological heritage (Fig. b).

The plan of the building is unusual. Whether the rooms on the west side belonged to the temple is not clear. It seems certain that the main structure is a temple with the distinctive columns and altars, but the rooms to the west had floors which contained domestic debris on them so they might have been the living quarters of the temple officials, rather than the sacred part of the temple. The columns could have supported

Fig.b. The temple after reconstruction

a roof or they might have been freestanding, it is very difficult to tell for certain.

The closest parallel to this building is provided by the temple at Saar, of roughly the same date, which has circular columns in the cella and some circular and rectangular structures outside rather similar to those at Diraz. In this case, the excavators have chosen to interpret them as offering tables rather than as structural columns (Crawford et al 1997). The columns on the inside of the cella at Saar would have supported the roof. The two altars in the temple at Saar are rather different in shape to those we found at Diraz. It is interesting that many of the sites of this period that have been excavated in Bahrain seem to have had a religious function: the Barbar temple (Anderson 1986), and the wells at Umm al-Sejour (Bibby 1972 & Konishi 1994), as well as the temples at Saar and Diraz, suggesting that religion played an important role in the life of Dilmun.

Behind the temple cella at Diraz East were the remains of a tomb [6]. It was much damaged by pits and only fragments of the structure were preserved. In 1973/4 Tony McNicoll dug the western part and in 1976 we excavated the remainder and found a pile of human bones in the north-east corner. The number of different bodies is difficult to establish because of the poor condition of the bone, but Shirley Jarman, who studied the bones from the tomb, thought that there were about 35 different individuals present, including babies, children, adolescents and adult males and females (Jarman 1977). Beneath the floor of the part of the tomb, where the bones were, was a layer of small seashells, but there were none under the floor next to the entrance to the tomb. The shells seem to have been put there to purify the area of the tomb itself. Although the tomb had been much disturbed there were some objects still in-situ: a bowl that could be probably dated to the Achaemenid Period, two stamp seals (Fig. c) again to be dated to the middle of the first millennium BC, some bronze/copper rings and a few stone and other beads. It seems likely that the tomb originally had an outer chamber in which the latest burial would have been laid and an inner one where the earlier burials would have been piled up as the tomb got re-used over several generations.

The closest parallel to these communal graves at Diraz East is provided by two tombs at the site of A'ali East near the centre of the northern half of the island (Map). Here the tombs were better preserved, although partly destroyed by pits, robbed and disturbed in later times. The first of these tombs, Tomb A, was excavated in 1976 and had two chambers and an entrance at the east end of the south wall. It was very much disturbed and later re-used in the Hellenistic period when a stone lined grave was inserted into the west end of Chamber 1 (Fig. d). All the human bone had been thoroughly chewed up and there was hardly a bone longer than about 5cm but according to Shirley Jarman these pieces probably represent the remains of more than 40 individuals. The pottery was slightly earlier than the objects from the Diraz tombs, perhaps belonging to the 7th or 6th century BC. Amongst the finds were fragments of bronze bowls, a Mesopotamian cylinder seal, which probably dated to the 7th century BC (Fig. e), a 'Persian Gulf' stamp seal (Fig. f), and a double sided green stone stamp seal (Fig. g), both of which must certainly have been heirlooms.. The double-sided stamp seal had a design of ibex headed people on it like those on a double-sided stamp seal from Susa dated to about 4000 BC (Amiet, 1980 no. 119 on p. 253), but it is probably to be dated to the Middle Dilmun Period like the two-sided seals found in Failaka (Kjaerum 1983 nos 336-366) whose style and composition closely match the seal from the tomb.

Fig.d General view of Tombs B and A at A'ali East

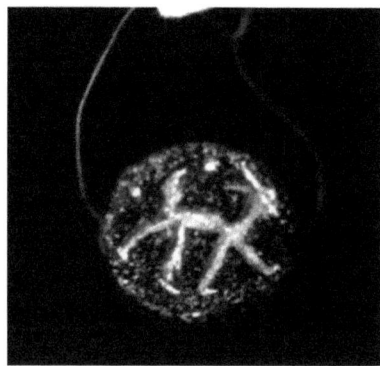

Fig. c. Stamp seal from Tomb (6) at Diraz East

Fig.e. Mesopotamian Cylinder seal from Tomb A at A'ali East

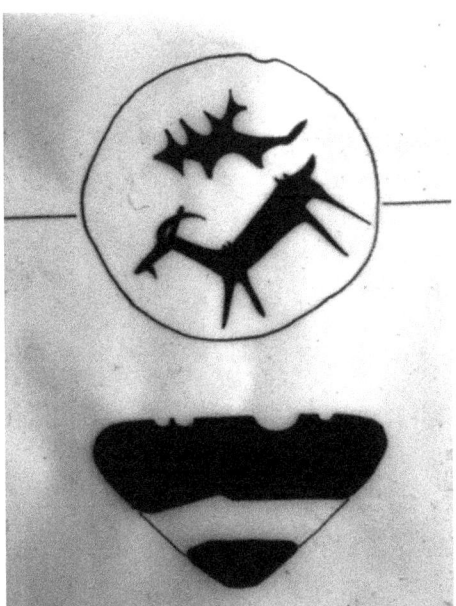

Fig.f. 'Persian Gulf' stamp seal from Tomb A at A'ali East

Fig. h. Early Dilmun seal from a pit dug into Tomb B at A'ali East

Fig.g. Middle Dilmun two sided stamp seal from Tomb A at A'ali East

The second tomb, Tomb B, excavated in 1977/8, was probably in use slightly earlier than Tomb A. and was better preserved. In the outer chamber some pottery vessels and a bronze bowl were associated with the final burial, while in the inner chamber the remains of the previous burials had been piled up. In the outer chamber the bones of the final corpse had almost entirely disappeared, but in the inner chamber we found a great heap of bones, including some 16 skulls and 38 femurs. Because of the later pits we think these bones represent about half the number of individuals, about 40 people, originally buried here. In amongst these bones eight fragments of bronze bowls and a gold ring were found, while a very beautiful Early Dilmun seal was recovered from an Islamic pit dug into the end of the tomb (Fig.h).

To sum up, the excavations of the British Archaeological Expedition to Bahrain uncovered the remains of an unusual religious building at Diraz East belonging to the early centuries of the second millennium BC. This temple has similarities with the temple excavated at Saar (see below) but with its open plan and forest of columns or circular platforms gives a quite different impression to the enclosed single room temple at Saar. The carefully constructed channels for draining away liquid from the altar suggest that sacrifices were carried out in the temple. The three mid first millennium communal tombs found in Diraz East and in A'ali East have no close parallels in the region Interestingly and unusually all age groups from new born to elderly and both men and women were buried in the same tomb. It is most likely that these tombs belonged to individual families and remained in use over several generations.

Acknowledgements

Again I would like to express my thanks to the Bahrain Department of Antiquities (especially to Shaikhah Haya al-Khalifa and Abdulaziz Swailih who co-directed the excavations at Diraz East and A'ali East respectively), to the sponsors of the British Archaeological Expedition to Bahrain, to the team members, and to the specialists who have helped with the analysis of the finds. I am also very grateful to Harriet Crawford for her assistance in editing this paper and for correcting my dating of the seals.

RESTRUCTURING BRONZE AGE TRADE: BAHRAIN, SOUTHEAST ARABIA AND THE COPPER QUESTION[1]

Robert CARTER

PART I: INTRODUCTION

This paper re-examines the great Bronze Age trading network of the Arabian Gulf and the Indian Ocean, focussing on the changing roles and interregional contacts of Bahrain and Southeast Arabia. There is already voluminous literature regarding the textual and archaeological evidence and the theoretical models underpinning this trade (e.g. Weisgerber 1986; Edens 1992; Possehl 1997; Edens 1993; During Caspers 1992; Potts 1992). A reappraisal is due in the light of recent evidence concerning Bahrain's relationship with the Late Harappan world, and new data regarding the origins of copper found within the orbit of the Bronze Age trading network. This paper is concerned with structural change during the later history of the Bronze Age Gulf trading network, rather than its genesis during the Early Dynastic period of Mesopotamia during the mid 3rd millennium BC.

Since Oppenheim's work (Oppenheim 1954), a generally accepted model of Bronze Age trade in the Gulf has emerged. From ca. 2500 BC there was a maritime trading system running between Southern Mesopotamia and the Indus region (including Gujarat). The major phase of interaction finished between 1800 and 1700 BC, at around the close of the City II period in Bahrain (Carter forthcoming). This is approximately coincident with the end of Rojdi C, Lothal B and Rangpur IIB/C phases in Gujarat, and the Jhukar phase in Sindh, which ended by ca. 1700 BC (Figure 1. See Possehl and Rissman 1992: 486; Mughal 1992: 216). Some authors have suggested that civil unrest in Southern Mesopotamia and the destruction of the city of Ur during the second half of the 18th century BC had terminal consequences for the Gulf maritime trading system (e.g. Reade 1986: 330).

During the 3rd millennium, maritime trade through the Gulf had become increasingly important, perhaps stimulated by burgeoning Mesopotamian demand during the Early Dynastic period, hostility between Mesopotamia and Elam, and the collapse of the Middle Asian urban system during the second half of the 3rd millennium (Possehl 1996: 189; Edens 1992: 132-133; Cleuziou and Tosi 1989: 42). Evidence from Ras al-Jinz, that boats built from wooden planks may have augmented reed-bundle boats at around 2300 BC (Cleuziou and Tosi 1997: 69), perhaps indicate that technological advances favoured the growth of the maritime route.

Southeast Arabia and Bahrain were incorporated into this network. In the Mesopotamian texts, "Dilmun" is thought to equate to Bahrain and adjacent regions in Eastern Arabia, as well as Failaka after 2000 BC (Possehl 1996: 135; Potts 1990a: 292). "Magan" is said to equate to Southeast Arabia, while "Meluhha" refers to the Indus region. Southeast Arabia is said to be an important supplier of copper to Mesopotamia throughout this period, and it has also been suggested that copper was exported from Southeast Arabia to the Indus region during the Bronze Age (Ratnagar 1994: 122; Weeks 1999: 53; Cleuziou and Tosi 1989: 42). Not all commentators agree with the latter viewpoint (Chakrabarti 1998: 311). Dilmun, Magan and Meluhha enjoyed direct trading relations with the 3rd millennium Akkadian and Ur III states (e.g. Potts 1990a: 135-149).

Dilmun came to monopolise the trading network by around 2000 BC, becoming the major or sole focus of exchange for goods from all parts of the maritime interaction sphere, while Magan and Meluhha disappear from the Isin-Larsa period economic texts. At this time, goods which could only have originated in the East are shipped through Dilmun, including copper, sometimes in very large quantities, which is usually assumed to come from Southeast Arabia (e.g. Potts 1990a: 219-224). One transaction relating to the Dilmun trader Ea-nasir records a sum total of over 18 tons of copper. After ca. 1800 BC, Mesopotamia turned to alternative copper sources in Anatolia and Cyprus (Crawford 1996: 16; Edens 1992:132; Weisgerber 1986: 139).

The identification of Dilmun with Bahrain and adjacent areas is accepted in this analysis, as is the role of Dilmun as the middleman of Gulf and Indian Ocean maritime trade during the early second millennium. The identification of Magan with Southeast Arabia is more contentious, and is based largely on the perception that Magan, like Southeast Arabia, appears to be a source of copper (see e.g. Glassner 1989: 182). In fact, the arguments for Magan's location in Eastern Iran and/or the Indo-Iranian borderlands are also strong, not least because of the evidence of copper mining in those areas (see below). Moreover, the famous Booty of Magan is of Iranian origin (Potts 1986: 280-284; Potts T. 1994: 235 and note 103). The term may refer to both regions (e.g. Possehl 1997: 89).

Inland routes and complex cross-relationships between the different regions continued to exist alongside the flourishing maritime trade (During Caspers 1992: 9). These were not parallel or supplementary routes, but were closely integrated with and intrinsic to the maritime trading complex. Overland caravan trails running East-West and North-South remained active (Figure 2), and maritime routes were part of a much

---

[1] Many thanks are due to the Bahrain-British Foundation for funding this research; to the London-Bahrain Archaeological Expedition and the Bahrain National Museum for their co-operation in giving access to the material from Saar and elsewhere; to Lloyd Weeks for his invaluable comments on this paper; and to Harriet Crawford for her unstinting support and advice

BC	Mesopotamia	Saar Pottery Period	Qala'at al-Bahrain	Failaka	South-east Arabia	Indus Region
1700	Old Babylonian		IIF	3A		
1750						

1800		4			Middle Wadi Suq Period	Lothal B Rojdi C Rangpur IIB-C
1850				2B		
1900	Isin-Larsa	3	IIc			
				2A	Early Wadi Suq Period	
1950						
		2		1	--------	
2000	--------		IIb			--------
2050	Ur III	1	IIa			
2100	--------		Ib			
2150			Ia			
2200					Umm an-Nar Period	
2250	Akkadian					Mature Harappan
2300						
2350	--------					
2400						
2450	ED III					
2500						

Figure 1: Chronological Table

larger network, which extended through both Iran and the Indus valley, deep into Central Asia (Possehl 1996: 182).[2] Work in Kerman has shown the importance of North-South interrelationships, stretching from Central Asia through Southeast Iran and across the Gulf to Southeast Arabia (Salvatori and Tosi 1997: 1997: 122). Routes originating in Central Asia would have met the Gulf through Southeast Iran (During Caspers 1992: 9; Weeks 1999: 61; Weeks 1997: 68), following a path via the Hilmand basin and the Bampur Valley towards the location of modern Bandar Abbas. From Kerman one could also journey directly South to this area. Hakemi (1997: 117) suggests this route from Kerman to the Gulf. Overland routes from Bandar Abbas to the North, East and West may be found along river valleys through the mountains. Important Bronze Age sites almost certainly remain to be found near Bandar Abbas, in the coastal zone and on the adjacent islands of Hormuz and Qeshm. From there it is a short sea journey across the Straits of Hormuz to Southeast Arabia or Bahrain. The Fars region in South-Central Iran, home of the ancient state of Anshan, may have had access to the Gulf through Bandar Bushire, a port conveniently en route between Bahrain and Failaka.

The movement of artefacts through, from and into the Dilmun orbit is usually thought to constitute evidence for trade

---

[2] For a historical outlook see Chakrabarti (1998: 307, 311-312). A useful map is provided by Lahiri (1992, Map 12).

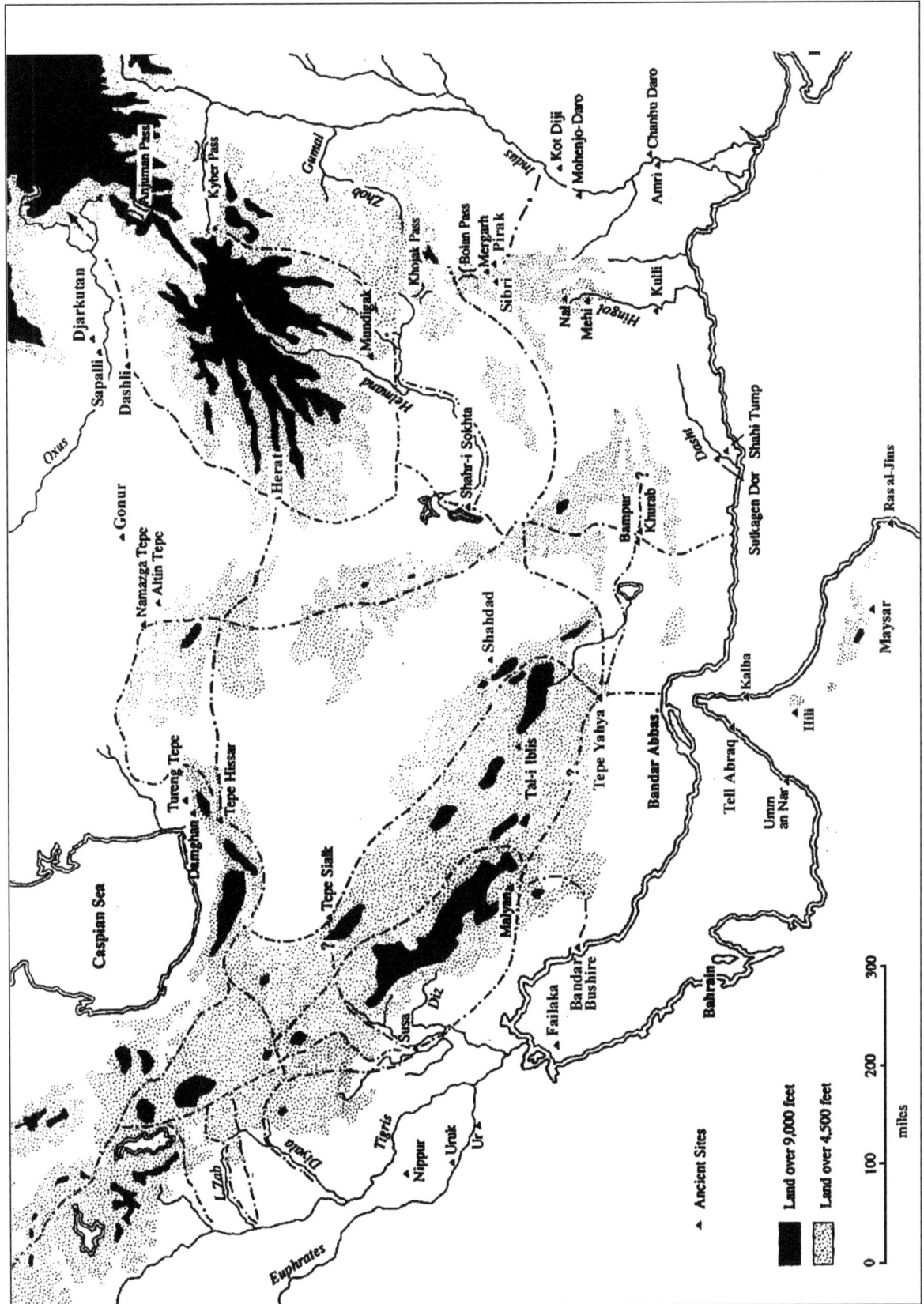

Figure 2: Map of Major Routes and Sites (adapted from Potts T. 1994 fig. 5)

although other factors such as diplomatic relations, elite marriages, political clientship and warfare may also have played a role (Edens 1992: 120-121). Particular consideration should be given to the sharing and emulation of traits from external cultures; such phenomena frequently indicate more fundamental and structural relationships than purely mercantile exchange. Some authors believe that emulation indicates unequal centre-periphery relationships (see e.g. Rowlands 1987: 4; Kohl 1979: 80; During Caspers 1989: 14. Edens 1992: 127-129), though the theory that societies in the Gulf became dependent on Mesopotamian barley has been questioned (Potts 1992: 424-425).

PART II: REVIEW OF THE ARCHAEOLOGICAL EVIDENCE FOR INTER-REGIONAL EXCHANGE

Dilmun and the Harappans

The Harappan civilisation played a formative role in the emergence of Bahrain's mercantile tradition. The inhabitants of Bahrain adopted the Harappan weight system. Seven weights conforming to the Harappan series are known from Qala'at al-Bahrain, mainly in City IIa layers, with others found at Saar (Højlund and Andersen 1994: 395-396). The value of a Dilmun standard measure, calculated according to ratio given in an Isin Larsa text from Ur, was found to correspond exactly to a unit in the Harappan system (Possehl 1996: 174-175).

Harappan script and motifs are found on Persian Gulf seals (Edens 1993: 346; Cleuziou 1992: 93; Tosi 1993: 372) which are associated with the 3rd millennium. The script was used to write non-Harappan words or names, suggesting its adoption and adaptation by local traders in the Gulf (Edens 1993: 346). This is further evidence for the emulation of Harappan practices, specifically those relating to the administration of economic affairs (Edens 1993: 353).

Following the turn of the millennium, continuing contact with the Indus region is demonstrated by the presence of Late Harappan pottery at Qala'at al-Bahrain and Saar. There are good indications that mercantile exchange between Qala'at al-Bahrain and the Indus sphere was more intense during the City II period than the City I period, with significantly greater quantities of Indus-related pottery, though the total amount is never high. Only 0.2% of the assemblage during the City I period is "Pottery in The Eastern Tradition". It peaks at 1.6% during the City IIa period, dropping to 1.1% by the City IIc period. Of this 'Pottery in the Eastern Tradition', four types are of purely Indus-related origin and have chronological significance. These are E1, E2, E7, E8, as well as a selection of sherds from his miscellaneous types E9 and E10. Two of these types are associated with period I and amount to a total of just 5 sherds: these are E1, a micaceous black-slipped ware probably comparable to the black-slipped Indus ware commonly found in Southeast Arabia; and E2, a brownish cord-impressed ware. Types E7, comparable to early second millennium post-Harappan Jhukar ware of the Indus valley, and E8, comparable to Late Sorath Harappan ware from Gujarat, are both assigned to Period II. They amount to a total of 23 sherds. The latter appears at the Qala'at only during the City IIc period, which complements the evidence from Saar that connections with Gujarat are strongest at that time (see Højlund and Andersen 1994 figs. 389 and 390; Carter in press).

At Saar a number of sherds comparable to Late Sorath Harappan and possibly Jhukar ware have been found (Carter in press). Although these are quantitatively negligible compared to the local pottery, they are the most common variety of imported pottery at the site. They are mainly large storage jars, and are comparable to Late Harappan ceramics from Lothal B, Rojdi C and Rangpur II B-C, and are associated with Saar Periods 2 and 3 (cf. Qala'at City IIb and IIc), being effectively absent from the latest phase of occupation at Saar. They show that Indus-related material penetrated not just the urban heart of Dilmunite Bahrain, but also smaller sites. Connections are also evident between Failaka and the Late Harappan sphere. An Indus-related sherd from Failaka Period 1 (Højlund 1987: 100-101 and fig. 435), and a series of seals have parallels at Pirak and Chanhu-Daro (Edens 1993: 347).

In Gujarat, a Dilmun seal was found at Lothal in unstratified deposits (Rao 1985 fig. 38A: 4) perhaps indicating the presence of Dilmun merchants at that site; a Dilmun-related seal has been reported from Dwarka (Crawford 1998: 90, Fig. 5.7). Otherwise, Dilmun artefacts are not known from Harappan and Late Harappan sites.

Dilmun and Iran and Central Asia

Separating influences and imports from the Harappan sphere, Eastern Iran, the Indo-Iranian borderlands and Central Asia is difficult owing to the complex interactions between these regions. There are numerous shared artefactual forms and styles. It appears, however, that contacts between Dilmun, Iran, and the borderlands have been underestimated. 3rd millennium connections between Dilmun and Eastern Iran, direct or otherwise, are demonstrated by Black-on-Grey pottery at Tarut and Abqaiq (Zarins 1989: fig 6:16, fig 11:6). Other connections with the Indo-Iranian borderlands are suggested by a so-called Kulli mirror handle from the late 3rd millennium Barbar Temple IIa, whose nearest comparison is with a mirror from Mehi (Possehl 1996: 173-174).

Attention has been drawn to parallels within the Murghabo-Bactrian complex (MBAC) of Central Asia (During Caspers 1992: 10), which flourished in Margiana (Southern Turkestan) and Bactria (Northern Afghanistan) between ca. 2100 and 1750 BC, but which also appears to become established in the Indo-Iranian borderlands (During Caspers 1996: 47-49; During Caspers 1994: 33-34). During Caspers has discerned further MBAC links in the pedestalled goblets, frequently with a ridge between cup and stem, which are found in the burial mounds of Bahrain and the Saudi mainland (During Caspers 1994: 34-41). Additionally, Højlund and Andersen's type E6, which occurs only in Periods IIa and IIb, can be compared to pottery from Mehrgahr VIII (Højlund and Andersen 1994: 120 and figs 340-347). A handful of seals from Bahrain also relate to the Central Asian and/or Indo-Iranian traditions (Crawford 2001: 31; Crawford and al-Sindi 1995).

MBAC prototypes may have either been directly copied, or transmitted via the Harappan or Indo-Iranian assemblages. A case in point is a chalice from the Saar tumulus 140, which is said to have Harappan parallels at Mehrgarh, but have its prototypes in Bactria, in the tombs of Dashly Tepe 3 (Lombard 1999: 99, no. 98).

Relations with Fars in South-Central Iran are demonstrated by the presence of Kaftari Buff Ware vessels at the Qala'at, at Tarut, in Failaka and in a tomb from Dar Kulayb, Bahrain (Højlund 1987: 100, fig. 432-434; Højlund and Andersen 1994: 118-119, figs. 332-337). The Tarut example is described as "Buff Ware" (Zarins 1989 fig. 6: 20). The one from Dar Kulayb (Lombard 1999: 96, no. 94) is described as being "dans le style de l'Indus". Both of the latter bear pipal-leaf decoration, hence the comparison with Indus pottery, but the paste, shape and decoration of multiple parallel straight horizontal lines below the rim, with a single horizontal wavy line enclosed, indicate a Kaftari origin. At the Qala'at, Kaftari sherds are coded E4, and occur in the late 3rd and early 2nd millennia, in periods Ib and IIb. At Failaka they fall into Period 1 (i.e. early 2nd millennium) while the Tarut example appears to be late 3rd millennium. Access to South-Central Iran may have been through Bandar Bushire, where a late 3rd/early 2nd millennium settlement produced Barbar ware, as well as Kaftari pottery, a bun-shaped copper ingot and *série tardive* (Wadi Suq style) softstone (Pézard 1914: Pl. V: 9; Pl. VIII: 2 and 16). Other sites along the Central Iranian littoral will certainly be found to contain Barbar pottery. For example, a typical Dilmun jar with a scored rim was observed by this author in the Williamson Collection, at the Ashmolean Museum. This was found near Taheri, some 200km SE of Bandar Bushire, ca. 240km NE of Bahrain. Additionally, a few beakers from Saar may relate to Iranian traditions (Carter forthcoming).

Locally made lugged canister jars, some bearing Iranian-influenced designs, have parallels at Susa in Khuzistan, underlining the Elamite connection (Lombard 1999: 64-65, nos. 34, 41). Further significant finds from Susa include four Dilmun seals, a sealing, a Dilmun seal impression and cylinder seals with Dilmun iconography (Potts 1999: 179; al-Gailani Werr 1986). There is also an unprovenanced Dilmun seal from Iran (Edens 1993: 347). An early 2nd millennium text from Susa details silver delivered by a Dilmunite (Potts 1999: 180). These occurrences show that trade with Western Iran was direct, rather than mediated through the rulers and merchants of Southern Mesopotamia.

Bitumen was one item of this trade. Compositional analysis of bitumen from a range of late 3rd and early 2nd millennium artefacts from Saar shows that it was exclusively imported from Khuzistan and/or Fars in Iran during the Early Dilmun period (Connan et al. 1998: 177). The same is true of the bitumen from tombs at Karanah and Buri. Material from Qala'at al-Bahrain, however, from both the late 3rd and early 2nd millennia and from a variety of artefacts, originated from Mesopotamia. Its composition closely matches that found at the third millennium site of Ras al-Jins 2 in Oman (Connan et al. 1998: 177). The difference in bitumen sources implies that the Saar, Buri and Karanah bitumen did not come via Qala'at al-Bahrain. Furthermore, there is a continuity of bitumen source at both Saar and Qala'at al-Bahrain from the late 3rd to early 2nd millennia, when political control of Susiana and possibly also Fars swung from the Ur III dynasty to the Iranian Shimashkians and then the *sukkalmah* rulers in Susa. These two inferences suggest that certain sites on Bahrain partook in a direct relationship with Western or Central Iran, in a cycle of exchange which was separate from that known to exist between Mesopotamia and the Qala'at al-Bahrain.

Dilmun and Southeast Arabia

Southeast Arabian-related material is found in Bahrain in both the third and second millennia. The quantity, type and context of this material are very different in each period, and suggestive of a changing relationship between the two regions. The nature of Bahraini material found in Southeast Arabia also changes.

Bahrain/Dilmun and Southeast Arabia in the late 3rd millennium

Nearly five hundred sherds of Umm an-Nar pottery are found at Qala'at al-Bahrain, City I period, with a handful from City IIa levels (Højlund and Andersen 1994: 111-117 and fig. 388). Isolated sherds of Umm an-Nar pottery are also found at Saar (Carter forthcoming). All are from the small painted jars that characterise the Southeast Arabian funerary assemblage. Such jars are common in late 3rd millennium tombs in Bahrain, with at least 24 vessels on display in the National Museum. Most are from Dilmun-style tombs in Hamad Town, and one is published (Srivastava 1991: fig. 54).

Umm an-Nar vessels are also found at the Tarut settlement and in tumuli at Abqaiq (Zarins 1989: fig. 6: 6, 12; fig 11: 1, 7, and possibly 12). This suggests that the mainland and Tarut shared a similar relationship with Southeast Arabia as Bahrain. As well as Umm an-Nar ceramics, Umm an-Nar style softstone vessels (*série récente*) are common in Bahrain (David 1996: 38 and Figure 1).

The nature of Early Dilmun's interaction with Southeast Arabia is obscure at this stage. The strong Umm an-Nar artefactual presence may represent either the emulation of Southeast Arabian funerary practices, the presence of Umm an-Nar visitors or colonists, or simply a trade in finished goods, namely painted vessels and/or their contents. Vogt discerns "an extension of the Umm an-Nar cultural sphere" into Bahrain (Vogt 1996: 109) and their is some evidence to back this up. A small number of tombs in Bahrain have strong architectural affinities with Umm an-Nar collective burials. They are circular, with internal compartments and an external plinth (Crawford 1998 fig. 3.2). Unfortunately, no information is yet available regarding their contents and dating. Should they turn out to be third millennium in date, they will comprise strong evidence of either the presence of a Southeast Arabian community within Bahrain at that time, or the adoption of Umm an-Nar burial practices by certain inhabitants of Early Dilmun.

It has also been suggested that the ashlar masonry seen at the Barbar temple owes its inspiration and technology to the Umm an-Nar culture (Crawford 1998: 73). Although the temple is unlike anything known from Southeast Arabia in conception and plan, the techniques of cutting and shaping ashlar masonry from limestone are, until the building of the Barbar Temple II, known in the Arabian Gulf only to the Umm an-Nar culture of Southeast Arabia. Given the abundant presence of Umm an-Nar pottery during the City I period in Bahrain, it is logical to infer that the techniques used at Barbar, and perhaps even the masons themselves, originated in

Southeast Arabia. There are chronological difficulties associated with this argument, however. The ashlar masonry appears at Barbar Temple II, but not before. Barbar Temple II correlates with Qala'at al-Bahrain City IIb, implying a date after 2000 BC, and therefore after the end of the Umm an-Nar period.

Qala'at City I material from Bahrain/Early Dilmun is almost absent from Southeast Arabia. Two sherds of chain-ridged ware are reported from Tell Abraq (Potts 1993a: 123). Chain-ridged sherds from Umm an-Nar island are thought not to be in Barbar ware, but may represent pre-Barbar antecedents from the Eastern Arabian mainland (Frifelt 1995: 152-153 and fig. 203). Abundant City II pottery, however, is found at Tell Abraq in very late third and early second millennium levels. These include up to 665 red-ridged sherds (Barbar ware), comparable to Bahrain's City II pottery and the Failaka assemblage (Potts 1991: 72-75 and fig. 96; Potts 1993a: 123). PIXE/PIGME analysis has revealed that the elemental composition of these Barbar sherds is comparable to that of sherds from Saar (Grave et al. 1996). The statement that they "originated in the ceramic workshops" of Saar is misleading, given the absence of evidence for pottery manufacture at the Saar. Bahraini pottery is also found in the tomb at Tell Abraq (Potts 2000: 121), dated to the last century of the 3rd millennium, coinciding with the very start of the Qala'at City II period and the end of the Ur III period in Mesopotamia.

Certain other Barbar vessels found in Southeast Arabia may relate to either the late 3rd or early 2nd millennium. Sherds of City II red-ridged Barbar ware were found at Khatt, in association with a raised "platform" (de Cardi et al. 1994: 44). In addition, a sherd from a Dilmun funerary jar with a scored rim (Højlund's Type B73) was found above a disturbed tomb at Khatt, with others at Shimal, Nud Ziba and associated with 3rd millennium tombs at Munayi and Kalba (de Cardi et al. 1994: 46; Kennet and Velde 1995 fig. 14; Méry et al. 1998: 169-171). A rim from a tomb in the Wadi Suq appears to be from a Barbar vessel, while Frifelt compares another sherd, from the Wadi Sunaysl, to pottery from Qala'at al-Bahrain (Frifelt 1975 fig. 21c and fig. 27c). An unpublished City IIc jar rim was also found outside the recently excavated tomb at Shimal, Unar2.

Dilmun seals are rare in Southeast Arabia. One was found in a Hafit period tomb at Mazyad (Cleuziou 1981 fig. 8) another has been identified in the tomb at Tell Abraq (Crawford 2001: 19), with a possible imitation from the settlement (Potts 2000: 122).

Bahrain/Dilmun and Southeast Arabia in the early 2nd millennium

In comparison to the 3rd millennium Umm an-Nar pottery, imported 2nd millennium Wadi Suq pottery is almost absent from Bahrain. It is not found in Failaka (contra Potts 1990a: 275-276), or identified at Qala'at al-Bahrain. Three sherds from Saar may have been imported from Southeast Arabia during the 2nd millennium (Carter forthcoming). One is a body sherd bearing a caprid motif, while the other two are rims from medium-sized jars. Their origin cannot yet be confirmed, but their paste and form identifies them as the only probable Wadi Suq pots known from Bahrain.

In the past, a Wadi Suq origin has been suggested for other Bahraini sherds (e.g. Larsen 1983: 247), but these are now known to be local. A type of painted spouted jar, bearing the design of pendant hatched triangles or concentric semi-circles between parallel lines, is an imitation of a well-known Wadi Suq painted spouted jar (Højlund and Andersen 1994: 176).

The motif of concentric semi-circles between parallel vertical lines, which was probably copied from Wadi Suq pottery, is also found occasionally on Bahraini necked jars, for example from Hamad town (Lombard 1999: 63, no. 26); it is also found on a bowl from Dhahran (Zarins 1989: fig. 14: 10). Other vessels from tombs in Dhahran show similarities with both Wadi Suq and Late Harappan beakers, though it is impossible to say whether they are local or imported (Zarins 1989 fig. 14: 5, 6). A few of the sherds from Højlund's types E9 and E10 (the Eastern Tradition) bear motifs compatible with the Wadi Suq assemblage (Højlund and Andersen 1994 figs. 362, 381, 383), but these are rare, the motifs are not exclusive to Wadi Suq pottery.

Second millennium Wadi Suq style softstone vessels (*série tardive*) are found within the Dilmun orbit, in lesser quantities than the Umm an-Nar style (David 1996: 39). It is unknown what proportion are imports, i.e. whether or to what extent local craftsmen imitated these styles. The same may be said of the numerous socketed spearheads found in Southeast Arabia and Bahrain during the early second millennium.

Some Barbar ceramics were making their way to Southeast Arabia during the early 2nd millennium. As well as the plentiful pottery from Tell Abraq mentioned above, a few Barbar body and rim sherds were found in the early second millennium levels at Kalba 4, but the overall quantity of Dilmun pottery at Kalba is very small compared to Tell Abraq (Carter 1997b).

Dilmun and Mesopotamia

For reasons of space, the following is not a comprehensive survey. Connections between the Qala'at al-Bahrain and Mesopotamia are strong during the 3rd millennium. Percentages of Mesopotamian pottery in Periods Ia, Ib and IIa are, respectively, 10%, 19% and 6% (Højlund and Andersen 1994 fig. 390). There is also evidence for relations between Mesopotamia and Eastern Arabia, with Akkadian to Isin-Larsa pottery on Tarut and at Dhahran (Zarins 1989: 81-82). Other important finds attesting to connections and trade with Mesopotamia include Persian Gulf and Dilmun seals at Ur, possibly the copper bull's head at Barbar, and cuneiform material from Qala'at al-Bahrain (Mitchell 1986: 283; Edens 1993: 347; Mortensen 1986: 184; Højlund and Andersen 1994: 168). It also appears that the Dilmunites emulated some Mesopotamian religious practices, evident in the architecture of the temples at Saar and Barbar (Moon et al.: 1995: 144; Andersen 1986: 175).

During the early 2nd millennium, Mesopotamian goods and influence are less evident in Bahrain. At the Qala'at, the percentage of Mesopotamian pottery drops to 0.8% and then 0.4% for Periods IIb and IIc (Højlund and Andersen 1994 fig. 390). Mesopotamian pottery is also extremely rare at Saar, and is found only in Saar Period 2, being absent from 3 and 4 (Saar Period I was not studied). The reduction in Mesopotamian goods in early 2nd millennium Bahrain is certainly due to the establishment of Failaka as Dilmun's main port of trade in the Northern Gulf. Connections with Mesopotamia, probably via Failaka, were maintained right to the end of the City II period, with Barbar pottery found in Old Babylonian contexts at Larsa (Méry et al. 1998: 166-169). Continuing connections are also evident in the iconography of Early Dilmun Style I seals, much of which appears to be derived from Mesopotamia, or perhaps Susa or North Syria (Crawford 2001: 26, 29-31)

PART III: COPPER SOURCES AND THE SOUTHEAST ARABIAN PROBLEM

As noted in the introduction, it is generally believed that Southeast Arabia was the major supplier of copper to Mesopotamia, and perhaps the Indus region, during the Bronze Age maritime trading phenomenon. It is also assumed that after ca. 2000 BC, when Magan disappears from the texts, Southeast Arabian copper was still "a staple of the trade" and was shipped to Mesopotamia through Dilmun (Edens 1992:132). Very large quantities appear to be shipped to Ur from Dilmun during the Isin-Larsa period.

The discovery of Bronze Age copper workings in the mountains of Oman swung the argument heavily in favour of the identification of Magan with Southeast Arabia. A smelting site of the late 3rd millennium has been excavated at Maysar 1, and other Bronze Age smelting areas have been identified in the Wadi Salh, Assayab, Bilad, Muaidin, Tawi Ubaylah, and Zahra (Hauptmann et al. 1988: 35). Copper was mined at Arjah and al-Bayda and smelted nearby at Zahra (Costa and Wilkinson 1987: 98). Although production at Maysar 1 is thought to have on a domestic basis, the size of slag heaps in the mountains of Oman indicates smelting on an industrial scale during the Umm an-Nar period (Hauptmann 1985: 114).

Copper was probably exported from the settlement on Umm an-Nar island, where both Harappan and Mesopotamian ceramics are plentiful (Frifelt 1995: 121), and which dates back to at least the middle of the third millennium. It includes a building interpreted as a warehouse, and is well placed to act as a trading post on the West Coast of Southeast Arabia. Following the abandonment of Umm an-Nar at around 2200 BC, Tell Abraq may have acted as Southeast Arabia's copper outlet, though no warehouses have been found. It should be noted that the goods passing through these sites, including copper, did not necessarily all originate from Southeast Arabia. Both Umm an-Nar and Tell Abraq are well positioned as staging-posts along the East-West route between Mesopotamia and the Indus region.

Potential Copper Sources

While focusing on Southeast Arabia's role as a copper producer, most commentators have failed to note the evidence for extensive copper-working in other regions (see Figure 3). South central Iran was also an important copper producer at this time. The large-scale extraction of copper from numerous mines in Kerman, during the 3rd millennium is now well established (Hakemi 1997: 116-117). Smelting kilns of the late third and early second millennia are found near Shahdad at site D, on a scale suggesting that it was "a centre for the export of metal products" (Hakemi 1992). Shahdad actually expanded during the closing centuries of the 3rd millennium and its cemetery shows that occupation continued up to 1800 BC, though the early 2nd millennium settlement is less urban in character (Cleuziou and Tosi 1989: 39; Salvatori and Tosi 1997: 123; Hakemi 1997: 118). Tepe Yahya was probably served by a nearby mine known as Sheikh Ali (Cleuziou and Berthoud 1980: 243). Such sources would have had access Southwards, and are no further from the Arabian Gulf than the mining areas of Central Oman.

Copper sources are also found in Central Iran, easily accessible to Anshan and thence the Gulf port of Bandar Bushire (fig. 3). This region appears to have been incorporated into the exchange network: the presence of Kaftari vessels within the Dilmun orbit is noted above, while evidence from Southeast Arabia for connections with Elamite Western and South Central Iran is found in Kaftari vessels from very late Umm an-Nar tombs at Tell Abraq (Potts 2000: 116-117) and Shimal (unpublished). Although there is little direct evidence for copper trade between Anshan and Dilmun, save the Barbar pottery and ingot at Bandar Bushire, this may be due to the comparative lack of fieldwork in the region. Hostilities between the rulers of South Mesopotamia and South Western Iran at this time may have caused a switch from overland trading relations between Fars and Mesopotamia to a maritime route, via politically neutral Dilmun. Shimashki began to resist the Ur III state during the reign of Shulgi, and hostilities continued into the Isin-Larsa period. Following this, Elamite rulers terming themselves *sukkulmah* campaigned intermittently against Isin and Larsa (Potts 1999: 130, 139-149, 160-171).

Other copper sources are found further the East. From these copper may have been transported either directly Southwards to the Gulf, or into the Harappan system. In the Indo-Iranian borderlands there are sources in the Chagai Hills, Northwest Baluchistan (Cleuziou and Tosi 1989: 42). This is a particularly interesting proposition, as Potts has identified the Chagai district as a potential source of stone for the Indo-Iranian alabaster vessels of the Booty of Magan (Potts 1986: 284). There is access from the Chagai Hills northwards to the Hilmand system, westwards towards Kerman and southwards towards the Bampur Valley. Access to the Indus system, however, would probably have entailed a more indirect journey to the North, before passing East and then South via the Quetta Valley.

It is possible that Mesopotamian scribes made no distinction between the peoples or products of Eastern Iran/the Indo-

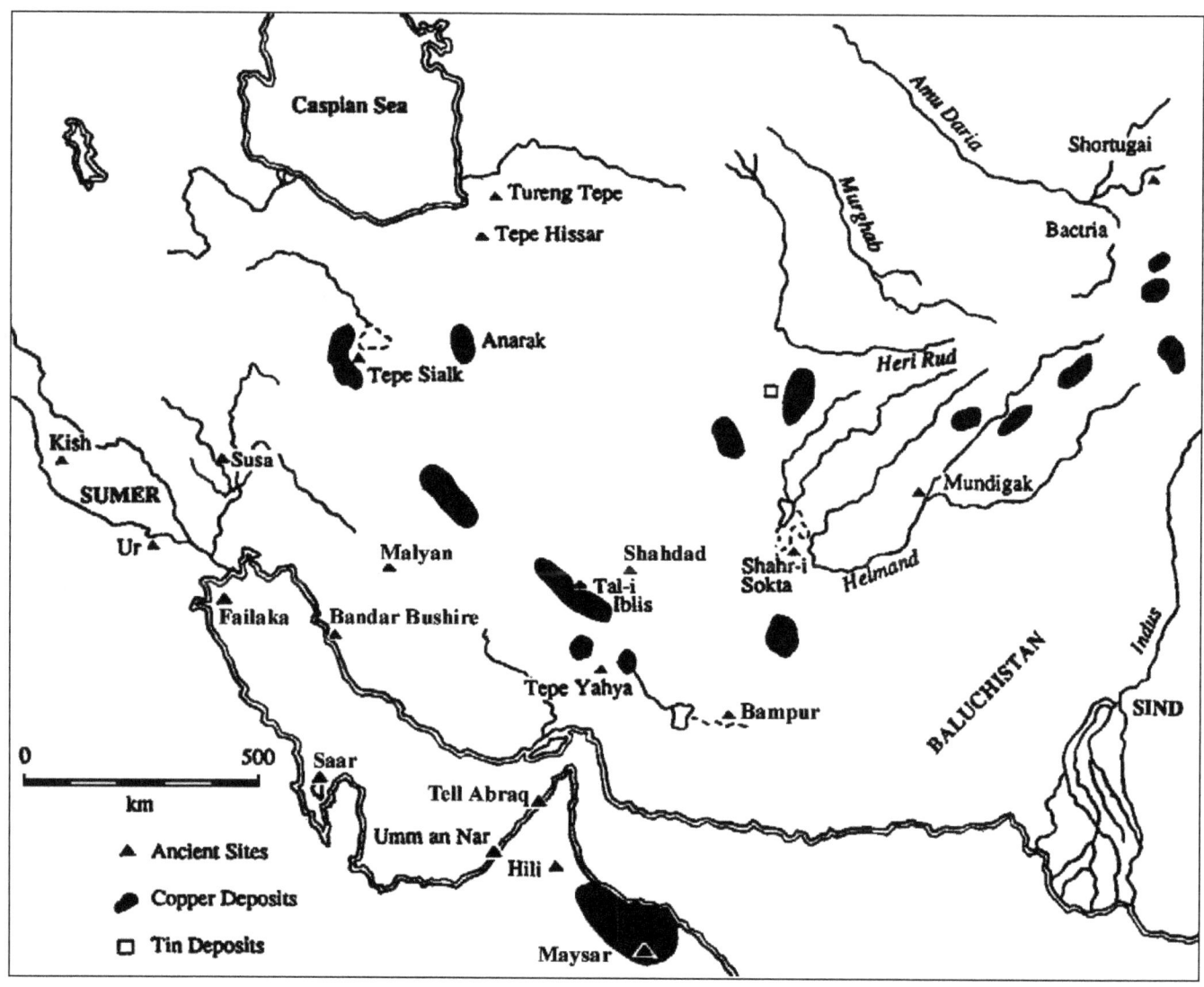

Figure 3: Map of Copper and Tin Sources (adapted from Potts T. 1994 fig. 21)

Iranian borderlands and Southeast Arabia, as the two regions maintained close cultural and possibly economic relations during the 3rd millennium. Umm an-Nar ceramics show long-standing and deeply rooted interaction with the Indo-Iranian borderlands (Edens 1993: 341; Frifelt 1995: 161-162). This bolsters the argument that "Magan" referred to regions on both sides of the Arabian Gulf (Possehl 1997: 89). These ties strengthen towards the end of the millennium (Salvatori and Tosi 1997: 131). Artefactual connections, probably indirect, are also evident between Southeast Arabia and Central Asia, either via the Indo-Iranian borderlands or the Harappan system (Potts 1994: 620-622; Vogt 1994: 122, 126, 129; During Caspers 1994: 37, 50; Salvatori and Tosi 1997: 124).

Copper may also have originated from sources within the Harappan sphere, or from adjacent areas of the Indian Subcontinent. During Caspers suggests that ores on the Deccan Plateau were exploited since the 3rd millennium BC, and increasingly supplemented the maritime traffic with Dilmun during the second millennium (During Caspers 1989: 21). There is abundant evidence of ancient copper extraction in Rajasthan, and copper bearing strata extend into the heart of Gujarat (Lahiri 1992: 107). The dating of the Rajasthani copper workings remains uncertain, though Lahiri reports a C-14 date of the last quarter of the second millennium BC for a mine in Udaipur (Lahiri 1992: 49). It is well-known that copper working of some kind occurred at Lothal, though this does not seem to have involved the smelting of ore. Rao is of the opinion that copper was purified at Lothal and then exported as bun-shaped ingots (Rao 1986: 379). Lead Isotope Analysis suggests, however, that copper from Rajasthan was not present at Tell Abraq or Saar (pers. comm. Lloyd Weeks).

Additionally, given the likely origin of the tin in the bronzes of Western Asia was Afghanistan (Weeks 1999: 60-61), it is possible that some copper originated from Afghanistan or Central Asia, and that un-alloyed copper as well as bronze was exported thence. Weeks suggests an overland route through Southeast Iran and across the Gulf of Hormuz to Tell Abraq and beyond for the tin and bronze, and it goes without saying that copper may have followed the same path (Weeks 1999: 61). The cost of transporting large quantities of copper over such a great distance overland would probably have been prohibitive, however. An alternative scenario has Afghani tin being alloyed in Iran or the Indus region with local copper.

Metallurgical Analyses

Several analyses have been attempted to establish whether Southeast Arabia supplied Mesopotamia with the bulk of its copper. Early results seemed promising. Peake identified nickel in various objects from the Northern Gulf, and pointed to the presence of nickel in ores from the mountains of Oman, in contrast to the absence of nickel in ores from Cyprus, Anatolia, Persian and Sinai (Peake 1928). Cleuziou and Berthoud found correspondences between the composition of mid and late 3rd millennium objects from the Northern Gulf and ores from Southeast Arabia (Cleuziou and Berthoud 1980: 243). They found correspondences between Omani ores and a "vase à la cachette" from Susa D, and "late third millennium objects from Ur".

Considerable doubt has now been cast on these results. A high nickel content is also found in certain ore sources in India (Chakrabarti 1998: 311). It has also been shown that Berthoud's analysis is based on too small a sample and his conclusions are questionable on geological and analytical grounds (Hauptmann et al. 1988: 34). In an analysis of ores from Oman and Iran using Sb/As and Co/Ni ratios, differentiation between the ores of the two regions was found to be practically impossible (Hauptmann et al. 1988: 42 and fig 4.9). It was concluded that "the final evidence that copper produced in Oman was used in Mesopotamia has not yet been given by analytical data", and that identification of Southeast Arabia and Magan still rested on the Mesopotamian texts and the evidence of smelting in Oman (Hauptmann et al. 1988: 49).

More recent and detailed analyses have also shown that the trade in metals, specifically copper, bronze and tin, is far more complex than previously acknowledged. Analysis of copper and bronze items from Tell Abraq has suggested that not merely the tin but also the copper to make the bronze was sometimes imported onto the site during the late 3rd and early 2nd millennia BC. It appears that both metallic tin and pre-alloyed bronze, from outside Southeast Arabia, were being circulated in the Gulf at this time (Weeks 2000: 259). 53% of the third millennium Umm an-Nar period objects chosen for analysis turned out to be tin-bronze, as well as 41% of those from the ensuing 2nd millennium Wadi Suq period (Weeks 1999: 53). This is a high proportion of imported metal, or alloy containing imported metal.

Moreover, of the copper objects subjected to Lead Isotope analysis, those dated prior to the mid-second millennium were incompatible with the Semail sulphide sources of the Oman Peninsula. Some may be compatible with the mantle-sequence rocks of the Omani ophiolite, though this is tentative (Weeks 1999: 56-57). It is quite possible that copper from Tell Abraq was derived from Omani sources which have not yet been subjected to Lead Isotope analysis, but the fact remains that proof has not yet established of a link between this metal and Omani ores. Weeks (2000: 262) is only prepared to speak of "a general isotopic similarity" between the analysed Southeast Arabian objects and samples from the mantle sequence. Interestingly, there was also very little overlap between data from copper from Saar, and the ore and slag data from Southeast Arabia (Weeks 2000: 262). No link can therefore yet be established between this Early Dilmun site and the region usually said to supply Dilmun with its copper.

Implications of the Metallurgical Analyses

The importance of these results cannot be underestimated. Firstly, they suggest that an important external source of bronze was supplying Tell Abraq during the 3rd and early 2nd millennia. Also significant is the fact that tin-bronze of any origin is rarely found in Southeast Arabia outside Tell Abraq, until the Iron Age (Weeks 1999: 53; Hauptmann et al. 1988: 47-48). Even the un-alloyed copper at Tell Abraq could not be linked to Southeast Arabian ores, though this is not conclusive proof that no Southeast Arabian copper was reaching the site.

These facts imply that the smelting areas in the Omani mountains were involved in a different exchange system to Tell Abraq, though an Omani source may still in theory have been supplying Tell Abraq and the Gulf system. Complementary evidence, however, supports the former scenario. A separation between an Arabian Gulf exchange system, in which Tell Abraq was involved, and a local system based around Southeast Arabian copper sources is wholly in accordance with what is known of Southeast Arabia's settlement patterns and interregional relations during the early 2nd millennium[3].

Patterns of settlement, copper production and cross-cultural affinities in Southeast Arabia differed radically during the 3rd and 2nd millennia. Hauptmann includes the Wadi Suq period in his estimate of copper production during the Bronze Age, and many or even all of the Bronze Age smelting areas identified might contain slag dating to that period. Copper was certainly smelted in Southeast Arabia at that time, especially in the light of the abundance of copper items in Wadi Suq tombs; it may even have been exported in small quantities. Nonetheless, unlike the Umm an-Nar period, there is a glaring absence of known Wadi Suq smelting sites or even sites showing secondary working of copper (Weeks 1997: 23). Recent assertions that there is evidence for "substantial Wadi Suq period mining in the Wadi Samad, Wadi Salh and on Masirah island" (Weeks 1997: 23 and note 139) are difficult to sustain. In the Wadi Samad and Wadi Salh such evidence is limited to the presence of Wadi Suq tombs or small quantities of cultural material in the vicinity of mining or smelting sites. On Masirah, no details are published other than that there is a mine with a provisional Carbon-14 date of the 18th century BC (Weisgerber 1988: 293, note 7).

Cleuziou and Berthoud have stated that "one cannot imagine a mining activity without local settled communities" (Cleuziou and Berthoud 1980: 239); by this reasoning, there

---

[3] This provides an interesting parallel with the results of bitumen analysis in Bahrain, described above, where the trading relationships of the major coastal conurbation appear to differ from those of the smaller "rural" settlements.

were insufficient people and infrastructure to carry out large-scale production in the Omani mountains during the early 2nd millennium. The interior of the peninsula was thinly populated from the start of the Wadi Suq period, and became progressively more so. Large settled communities became restricted to the coastal strips of the Northern parts of the Southeast Arabian peninsula and perhaps the Batinah Coast (Carter 1997a: 95-96). The existence of a few thriving coastal communities, at Tell Abraq and Kalba, does not alter that fact. Although tombs are found in the mining areas, settlements are not, and it appears that a fully sedentary lifestyle had been largely abandoned in those parts of Southeast Arabia. Copper mining and smelting by transhumant peoples is known to have occurred in Anatolia and Russia (Yener 2000: 83-84), but one would expect to find clearer archaeological traces if comparable communities were carrying out copper production on a large scale in Southeast Arabia.

Furthermore, although the archaeological evidence indicates that Southeast Arabia was closely involved in the interregional exchange system during the 3rd millennium, the evidence from the early 2nd millennium suggests isolation and lack of integration into the trading network. To summarise the 3rd millennium evidence, it appears that a strong Mesopotamian presence gave way during or after the Akkadian period to a phase of intensive interaction with the Harappans. Connections with Eastern Iran and the Indo-Iranian borderlands have already been noted above. Edens postulates that Southeast Arabia strengthened ties with the Indus civilisation in response to Akkadian imperialistic aggression in Iran and Southeast Arabia (Edens 1992: 133). Abundant Mesopotamian pottery and a seal impression at Umm an-Nar attest to trade with Mesopotamia and Syria during the Early Dynastic and Akkadian periods, and possibly the presence of foreign merchants (Frifelt 1995: 238-239 and Table 12). 3rd millennium Mesopotamian material is also found at Tell Abraq, Hili 8, Kalba and in various Umm an-Nar tombs (Méry and Schneider 1996: 83-84). Outside Umm an-Nar island, the quantity of Mesopotamian material never approaches that of Indus-related material during the later 3rd millennium, and Mesopotamian material is very rare throughout Southeast Arabia following the Akkadian period.

During the closing centuries of the millennium, a deep penetration of Harappan goods into Southeast Arabia is evident, as far as the copper-producing areas. These goods include weights (Potts 1990b: 41-42), seals (Cleuziou 1992: 97; Cleuziou and Tosi 1997: 63 and fig. 11:8 and 71 and fig. 11: 4, 7), beads (Vogt 1985: 33, Pl. 28: 4, 5; al-Tikriti 1989: 95, Pl. 58; Benton 1996: 126-128), metalwork (e.g. During Caspers 1994: 51; Frifelt 1995: fig. 276) and pottery (Vogt 1994: 159; Frifelt 1995: 129-130, fig. 178; al-Tikriti 1985: 13, Pl. 13B; Cleuziou 1992: 95-96; Potts 1993b: 328). Copies of Indus ceramics were occasionally made (Méry 1996: 171). To a lesser extent, Harappan mercantile practices were also emulated in that region: Indus weights are found at Tell Abraq, and locally made Harappan-influenced seals are found at Ras al-Jinz (Cleuziou and Tosi 1997: 71-71, fig. 11: 1, 2 5). These developments mirror the late 3rd millennium Harappan influence evident in Bahrain.

A dramatic change of emphasis is evident after 2000 BC, and it seems unlikely that Southeast Arabia as a whole continued to be integrated into the inter-regional exchange network. After the start of the 2nd millennium, the material culture of Southeast Arabia is very local in character. The strong cultural affinities between Southeast Arabia and the Indo-Iranian borderlands are terminated, due to the massive reconfigurations on the Iranian side of the Gulf during the last quarter of the 3rd millennium, with the collapse of urbanism first in Hilmand and then Kerman, and the apparently complete depopulation of Makran. There are some debatable artefactual indications of contact with the MBAC at this time (During Caspers 1994: 45, 50). The presence of tin-bronze at Tell Abraq demonstrates that material originating in Afghanistan or Central Asia was making its way to the Arabian Gulf, though it does not appear to have penetrated much further than Tell Abraq.

Mesopotamian pottery is rare, and virtually restricted to Tell Abraq (Potts 1992: 429, figs. 3, 4). A couple of Mesopotamian sherds possibly dating to the early 2nd millennium are found at Kalba, though they may also date to the late 3rd millennium (Carter 1997b: Part 8.4.1). Mesopotamian pottery is not found in Wadi Suq burials.

The Harappan input did not significantly or lastingly influence Southeast Arabian culture (Cleuziou 1992: 95, 99; Edens 1993: 354). Relations with the Late Harappan sphere are extremely limited, reduced to a small number of Jhukar or Late Sorath Harappan sherds from Tell Abraq, and a handful of occurrences in very early 2nd millennium tombs, including a cubical weight, pottery and etched carnelian beads (Potts 1994: 622-62; de Cardi 1988: 46, fig. 14; Vogt 1996: 113). Such finds may indicate that Southeast Arabia's retreat into isolation did not occur immediately at 2000 BC, though it appears to have happened rapidly during the first century of the millennium. This may partially account for the abundance of Barbar pottery at Tell Abraq in very early 2nd millennium layers. The contemporary settlement at Tawi Said in the Sharqiyah appears to lack imported material, and known foreign goods in Wadi Suq period tombs of the interior are limited to the two possible Barbar vessels from the Wadi Suq and the Wadi Sunaysl, mentioned above.

PART IV: CONCLUSIONS

To summarise, imported and copied materials show Bahrain enjoying a web of relationships during the 3rd millennium, to the East and Southeast (the Harappan sphere, Southeast Arabia, the Indo-Iranian borderlands, Central Asia) and the North and Northwest (Southern Mesopotamia, Susiana and Fars). Not all these relationships were necessarily direct, but the Mesopotamian and Harappan influence mentioned above and the presence of Umm an-Nar style graves implies that individuals from these three regions were present in Bahrain. The impact of the Eastern Iranian/Indo-Iranian influence is less clear-cut and its artefactual presence is small. The Harappans appear to have been the most influential visitors, and the emerging Dilmun culture was strongly influenced by the Harappan civilisation in the development of the mechanisms of trade, namely the system of weights and the use of seals. There is less evidence for the emulation of practices from other regions in Bahrain, though Southeast Arabia may have contributed to Early Dilmun's architectural and funerary practices.

The 3rd millennium expansion of various cultures in the Early Dilmun sphere agrees with the Akkadian and Ur III texts, in which various different regions (Dilmun, Magan and Meluhha) can be seen to be participating fully in the maritime trading network. The emergence of Dilmun at the start of the 2nd millennium as the main agent of trade is also supported by both texts and archaeological evidence.

Bahrain/Dilmun's relations after 2000 BC are oriented towards Mesopotamia, Susiana, Syria and possibly Fars to the North and Northwest; and the Late Harappan sphere to the East. There is an increase in Indus-related material, specifically in Late Sorath Harappan ceramics from Gujarat. This demonstrates that trade with the Harappans continued to be significant after the end of the Mature Harappan phase, putting the mercantile orientation of Late Harappan societies into a new perspective. A decrease in Mesopotamian material in Bahrain is due to the establishment of Failaka as Dilmun's northerly gateway to that region. Direct relations with Susa and possibly Anshan were maintained, with Bandar Bushire possibly acting as a staging post and trading centre, visited en route between Failaka and Bahrain. The processes of emulation in Bahrain were slowed as the Dilmun culture achieved maturity, except for the imitation of certain glyptic and ceramic styles; this is indicative of stylistic borrowing, but not structural change. There is no evidence for the activity of merchants from the regions with which Bahrain was in contact. These factors confirm the scenario given by the early 2nd millennium texts from Ur, which show Dilmun as the dominant trading power in the Arabian Gulf.

There can be little doubt that Southeast Arabia at least partially fulfilled Mesopotamia's copper requirements during the 3rd millennium. As well as the evidence of mining in the mountains of Oman, Southeast Arabia was well integrated into the Gulf exchange network from the Early Dynastic period until around 2000 BC. Even during the late 3rd millennium, however, Southeast Arabia would not have been the sole or even main contributor to the copper trade: the region's close cultural affinities with other copper-producing regions in Eastern Iran and the Indo-Iranian borderlands are noted above, and together these areas may have supplied a considerable quantity of the copper reaching Mesopotamia. Copper may also have been coming directly from the Harappan sphere: the texts regularly document copper from Meluhha (Possehl 1996: 145 ff.). As noted above, some authors believe the Rajasthani mines to have been active at this time (Dhavalikar 1997), though copper from these sources has not yet been identified in the contemporary archaeological record.

There is no evidence for bulk trade between Dilmun and Southeast Arabia during the early 2nd millennium, such as would be expected if Southeast Arabia was exporting large quantities of copper. As well as there being a marked paucity of imported artefacts in Southeast Arabia, no cultural or stylistic traits from the Dilmun civilisation or any other were absorbed by the Wadi Suq period population, as might be expected from an intensive trading relationship. The autochthonous character of the Wadi Suq culture and the lack of imported material throughout the region gives an impression of isolation thoroughly at odds with Southeast Arabia's hypothetical role as the provider of copper to the early 2nd millennium exchange network. This tallies with the absence of known 2nd millennium settlements and smelting sites in the copper-rich areas of the region. The region was not entirely isolated, however, as demonstrated by the probable Wadi Suq pottery at Saar, and Wadi Suq influence on Barbar spouted jars.

These factors underline the unique position of Tell Abraq, a site which was clearly an important port, with strong interregional connections, but which appears to lack any significant trading hinterland. The best interpretation is that Tell Abraq functioned as a vital staging-post for Dilmun merchant ships travelling between the Central Gulf and the Late Harappan orbit. The site should not be regarded as a major entrepôt, except perhaps during the late 3rd and at the very start of the 2nd millennium. The Barbar pottery at Tell Abraq is thoroughly domestic in character, consisting of small storage jars with the occasional cooking pot or jar suitable for carrying water (see Potts 1990b fig. 71: 1, 4, 5; fig. 76: 5; Potts 1991 fig. 96), a stripped-down assemblage that would be characteristic of visiting sailors from Dilmun.

The current paradigm, whereby Southeast Arabia was the major supplier of copper to Dilmun, is therefore not supported by the evidence, and the contribution of other copper sources must be considered. Central Asia is an unlikely source, given the distance required for overland travel. Although the ceramic evidence implies that Bahrain and Late Harappan Gujarat were trading partners, the latter does not appear to have been a source of copper. This raises the interesting possibility that copper was actually being shipped by the merchants of Dilmun to Gujarat at this time, though there is no hard evidence for this.

By a process of elimination, the Indo-Iranian borderlands, Eastern Iran and Fars are contenders in the search for Dilmun's early second millennium copper sources. In Iran, Kerman was still a potential source of copper, notwithstanding widespread upheaval and depopulation in Eastern Iran and the Indo-Iranian borderlands towards the end of the 3rd millennium. Unfortunately, little is known of the archaeology of the source areas in Baluchistan, such as the Chagai Hills. Metal from sources in Fars may have entered Dilmun's trading circuit at Bandar Bushire, as part of a trading relationship between Dilmun and Anshan.

It is likely that Dilmun gathered its copper from a variety of sources during the early 2nd millennium. There were vast and complex trading networks through and leading to the Arabian Gulf during both the 3rd and 2nd millennia BC. These involved many different trading partners and resource areas. On occasion, discrete mercantile sub-systems can be discerned, for example in Dilmun's bitumen trade with Iran, or in Tell Abraq's high proportion of imported tin-bronze. Although the orientation of maritime trade appears simple during the early 2nd millennium, with Dilmun acting as the dominant middle-man, the structure of interregional relations was still far from linear. Dilmun undoubtedly enjoyed relationships, both direct and indirect, with many regions. Given that the very basis of an entrepôt's existence and wealth is its ability to pool material from several sources and deliver it to specific markets, the rise of Dilmun at around 2000 BC may relate directly to its ability to concentrate material from many areas. Its strategic location, cosmopolitan outlook and extensive inter-regional connections enabled it to satisfy Mesopotamian demand, and take over the dominance of Gulf trade previously enjoyed by the Harappans. Thus, Dilmun's ascent to trading pre-eminence may relate to the reduction or cessation of reliable copper supplies from traditional sources, such as Eastern Iran and Southeast Arabia, at the end of the 3rd millennium. Depopulation and upheaval in these areas may be important causative factors.

Major reconfigurations within the Harappan sphere were surely also involved in this process. The Mature Urban phase ended at around 2000 BC, and the vast Harappan area began to fragment culturally and economically. It is thought that merchants had played a critical role in the creation and regulation of Harappan society, comprising a significant sector of the ruling elite (Kenoyer 2000: 88, 99). As seen above, the role of the Harappans in the maritime trading system of the late 3rd millennium appears to have been very great. The disruption of the Harappan urban and commercial world at the close of the 3rd millennium BC, and a concomitant mercantile vacuum, may have provided the stimulus for Dilmun's rise to prominence. Trading relations with the East and other regions continued, and possibly even intensified, but now according to the terms of the merchants of Dilmun.

ARAD FORT, BAHRAIN: ITS RESTORATION AND FOREIGN RELATIONS

Archie WALLS

The restoration of Arad Fort took three and a half years. I worked on the project fulltime with between ten and a hundred plus workmen from India, Pakistan and Afghanistan. It was an exciting, interesting and satisfying project on which I used skills as architect, excavator, mason, carpenter and author of guides.

The identification of Arad Fort and its condition

Arad Fort is on the island of Muharraq, where the old capital of Bahrain was located. It is not part of the main island where the present capital, Manama, is situated. (Map)[1] The fort was constructed in around 1635, a date suggested by its first appearance on a Portuguese map. (Fig.1) In the Portuguese drawing Arad is shown as having outer and inner fortified squares each with corner towers linked by curtain walls with wall walks along the top. Dr Monique Kervran's[2] excavation in 1978 and my own between 1983 and 87 confirmed the existence of two fortified squares, one about 50metres in length and the other 30 metres - both with corner towers. (Fig.2)

When I first saw Arad it was in a state of near collapse due to erosion and the evaporation of the salt laden ground waters. Only the inner square was visible: its centre was completely filled by sand that sloped up to the top of the extant walls. The majority of its wall-head was lost. The base of the curtain walls was damaged by evaporation to a height of over 2 meters, and over 5 meters in the case of the west corner tower. The south tower had an added outer skin of masonry weighing about 400 tonnes, which had split down the centre and was moving downwards. At points around this outer skin's base its 2.5 metre thickness was reduced to some 25 cms, and was being levered outwards at the top where it was a 1 metre thick. Nevertheless on that my first day I was able to make interpretative sketches predicting the lost features, some of which were only proved when we had cleared all the sand from the interior two years later. One feature I did not anticipate was a fresh water moat despite having suggested the existence of a moat at the similarly constructed building of Al Tharmad on the Batina coast in Oman in the 1970s. This area was also fed by powerful aquifers. (Walls 1978)

The construction characteristics of the layered technique

Before I went to Bahrain, Sir Bernard Feilden first showed me photographs of Arad when we met in Edinburgh. The obvious characteristic of its construction was what I term the "layered technique". This layering is most visible when most of the external renders have fallen off a wall to reveal regularly spaced horizontal lines of render lying within the core material. One detail, best seen in section and which is characteristic of the technique, is found where the renders of adjacent layers overlap: the lower layer's render maintains its thickness around the corners and the higher layer's render is smoothed down over it to a slight point

The general construction principle is of a wall built up in layers of approximating the length of a man's forearm, 41-42 centimetres. Within each layer there are normally three courses of mud brick or stone. (Fig 3) Various materials have been used from hand made and box formed mud bricks with mud renders, to stone with harder renders. Once the three courses are laid a render is brought over the top surface and down both sides of the layer. This process of laying the bricks or stone and then rendering is then repeated again and again. In certain castles in Oman, instead of the three courses per layer, a single course of truncated conical or bucket-shaped mud bricks is used.

There are advantages to this construction technique. No scaffolding is required to apply a rendered finish to a wall's surface and if the protective render is damaged only a small area of the core material is exposed to the elements. Although at Arad, the building materials have a high salt content, if the renders are in good order, when the air temperature changes the consequent evaporation and production of salt crystals occurs only on the outside of the wall along the joints created by the overlapping renders. Consequently the salts are no longer a danger. However, the greatest benefit from the point of view of the restoration of Arad Fort is the fact that the layers enabled me to follow exactly the construction route taken by the original builders. This was essential if I were to make good the layers in a sequential manner, and I discovered that the layers moved around the fort's outer and inner walls in slow spirals.

The inner fortified square and its corner towers

The basic design of the inner square's four corner towers is the same. (Figs. 4/5) At ground level they have a diameter of eight and a quarter metres, which gradually reduces to seven metres at the battery level. The builders were well aware of geometrical relationships and if the outer faces of the flanking

---

[1] When I presented this paper at the Seminar I did not use notes and instead used slides as my own prompts, hence this text is based on a transcript made at the time. The following illustrations are taken from my book *Arad Fort, Bahrain: Its restoration, its history and defences*, published by the Ministry of Information, State of Bahrain, 1987.

[2] Dr Kervran kindly consented to my summarising her excavations in my book on Arad Fort. In 1978 she spent a few days at the site to establish north/south stratigraphical relationships with and examination of the outworks facing the estuary. Hers was the first reliable archaeological study of the site and confirmed the identity of Arad Fort with the fort in the Portuguese drawing.

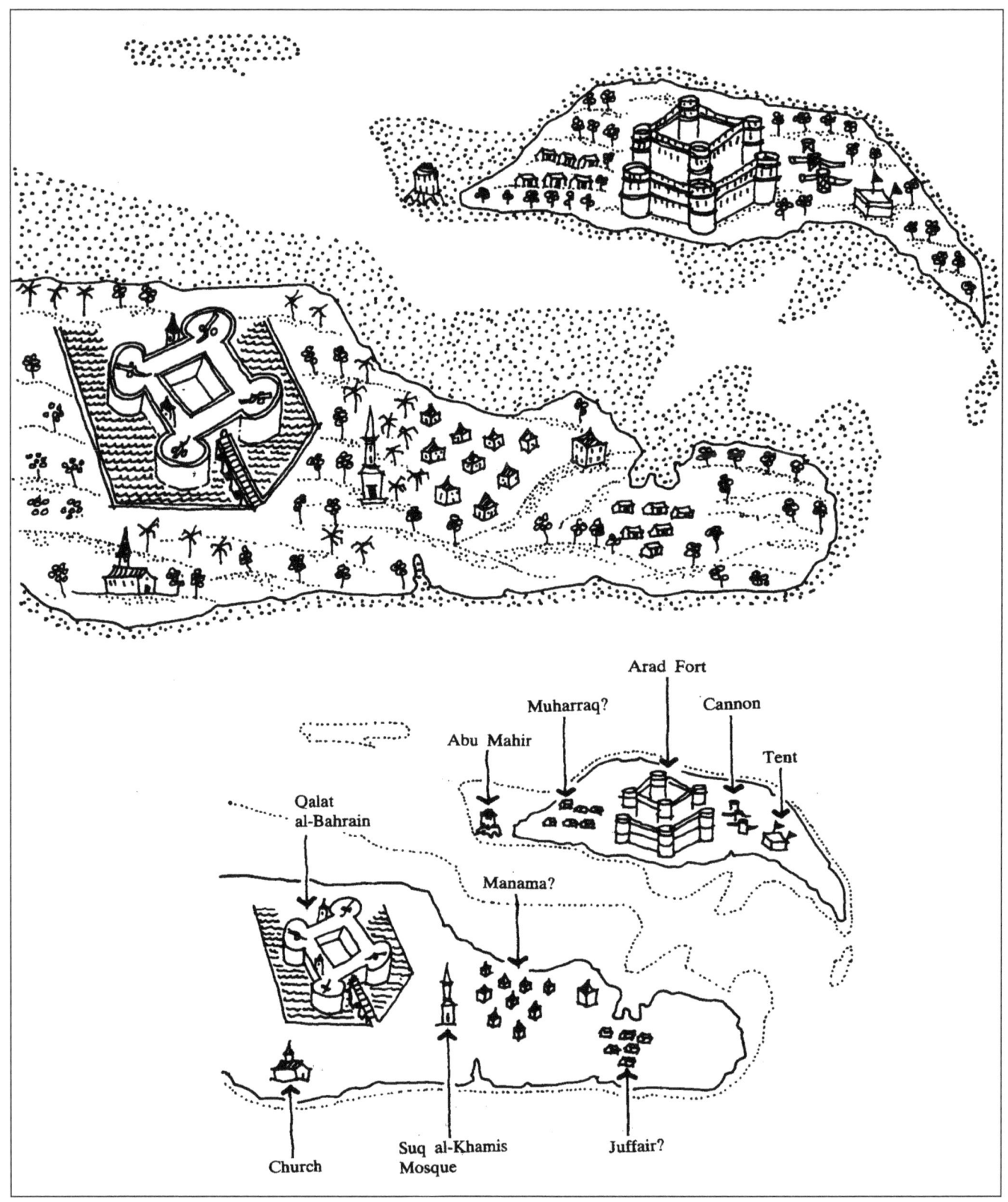

Fig. 1. Demonstracao da ilha de Baren circa 1635.

walls are produced they intersect at the centres of the towers. Each tower has palm trunk spokes and a platform at about the same level (Fig. 6), and it is probable that each had a central palm pillar. Although I was unable to confirm this last feature, there was evidence in a hole four metres long and thirty centimetres in diameter that a missing spoke in the west tower had left. Using a mirror to reflect the sun through this hole I was able to see a larger hole, like a chimney, at the centre of the tower. The palm spokes and platforms may have strengthened the towers, and palm being a fibrous wood may also have assisted in absorbing shocks when firing small mortars from the towers, or that of cannon balls hitting the structure. Coincidentally, three cannon balls were discovered lodged in the east tower - as if each one had come from the three baskets containing cannon balls shown in the Portuguese drawing!

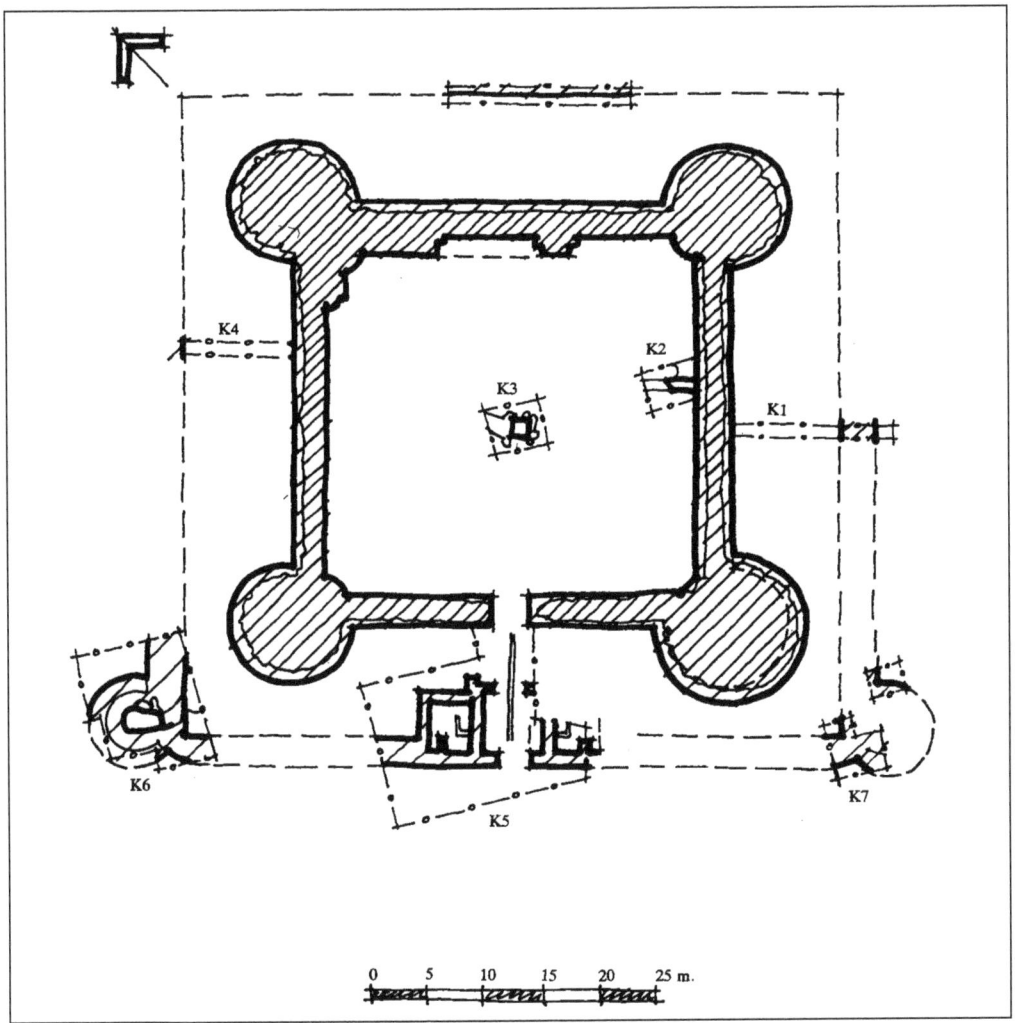

Fig. 2. Excavations carried out by Dr M. Kevran

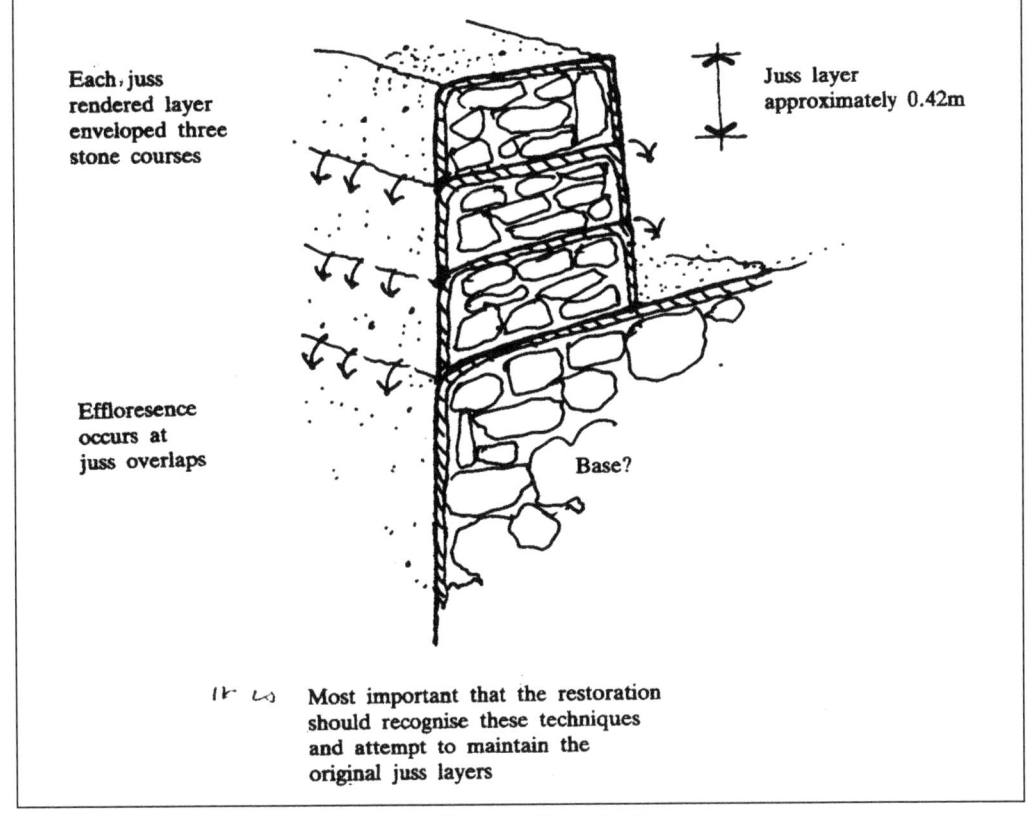

Fig. 3. Construction principles

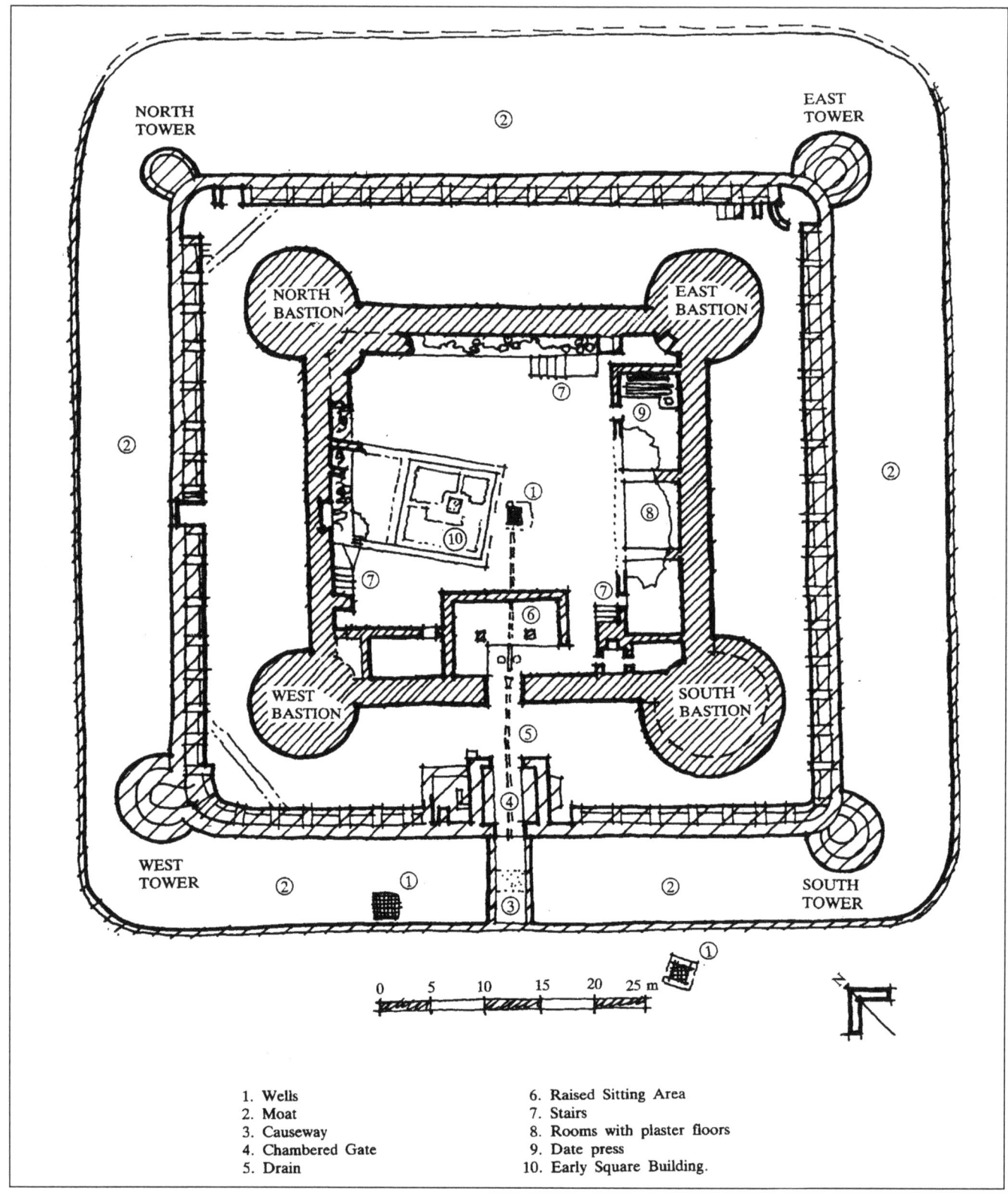

Fig. 4. Plan of the lower areas

1. Wells
2. Moat
3. Causeway
4. Chambered Gate
5. Drain
6. Raised Sitting Area
7. Stairs
8. Rooms with plaster floors
9. Date press
10. Early Square Building.

The original south tower was remodelled at some time to hold a cannon trained down the only navigable channel through the coral reefs protecting the entrance to the safe anchorage of Muharraq bay. (Fig.7) This remodelling entailed the addition of the outer skin, which I remarked earlier was in a state of collapse at the start of the restoration project in 1984. Before I arrived at Arad, the tower was thought to be too dangerous to work under, unless concrete was poured around the base to fill the gap and support the weight of the masonry. Had this been done the outer skin would have been destroyed within a few short years – cement and concrete are two of the enemies of historic buildings and their use should be avoided in restoration projects. As a result of the erosion and movement, the outer skin had broken into two halves with a vertical sheer crack at about the centre, which enabled it to continue its

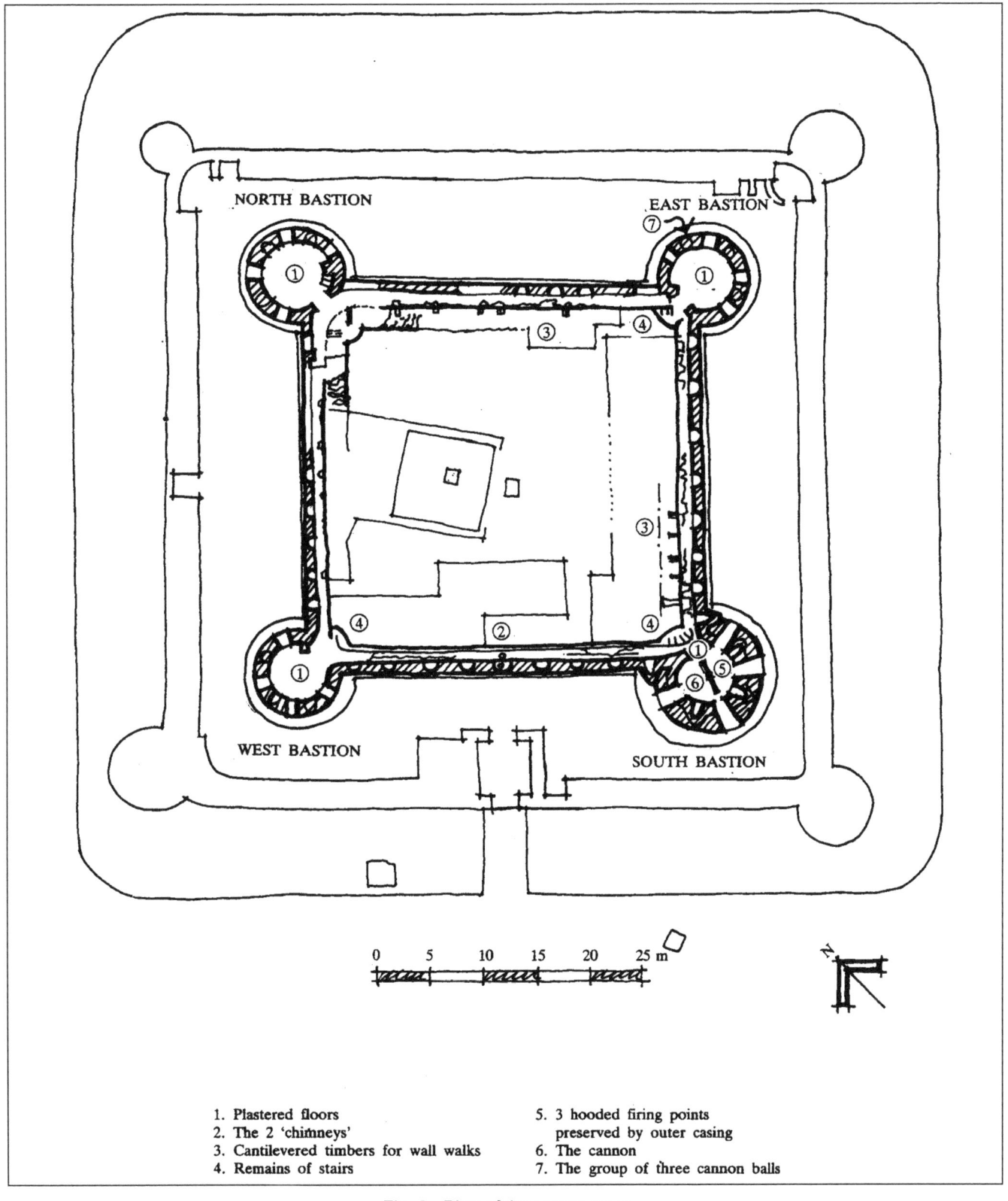

1. Plastered floors
2. The 2 'chimneys'
3. Cantilevered timbers for wall walks
4. Remains of stairs
5. 3 hooded firing points preserved by outer casing
6. The cannon
7. The group of three cannon balls

Fig. 5. Plan of the upper areas

downward movement over the increasing diameter of the original tower. Around the top of the tower the skin was being wedged outwards by the grains of sand lodged between the skin and the tower which progressively moved downwards whenever there was differential expansion and contraction caused by temperature variations. I shored up the outer skin and stopped the movement by inserting permanent resin bonded engineering brick shores around its base, which supported the skin's weight while we rebuilt the lowest courses. We used new layered masonry and renders that coincided precisely with the existing layers. (Fig.8) The majority of the sands and stones used in the reconstruction works at Arad came from my own excavations and clearing activities in and around the fort. Lime and gypsum were the only materials bought-in in any quantity.

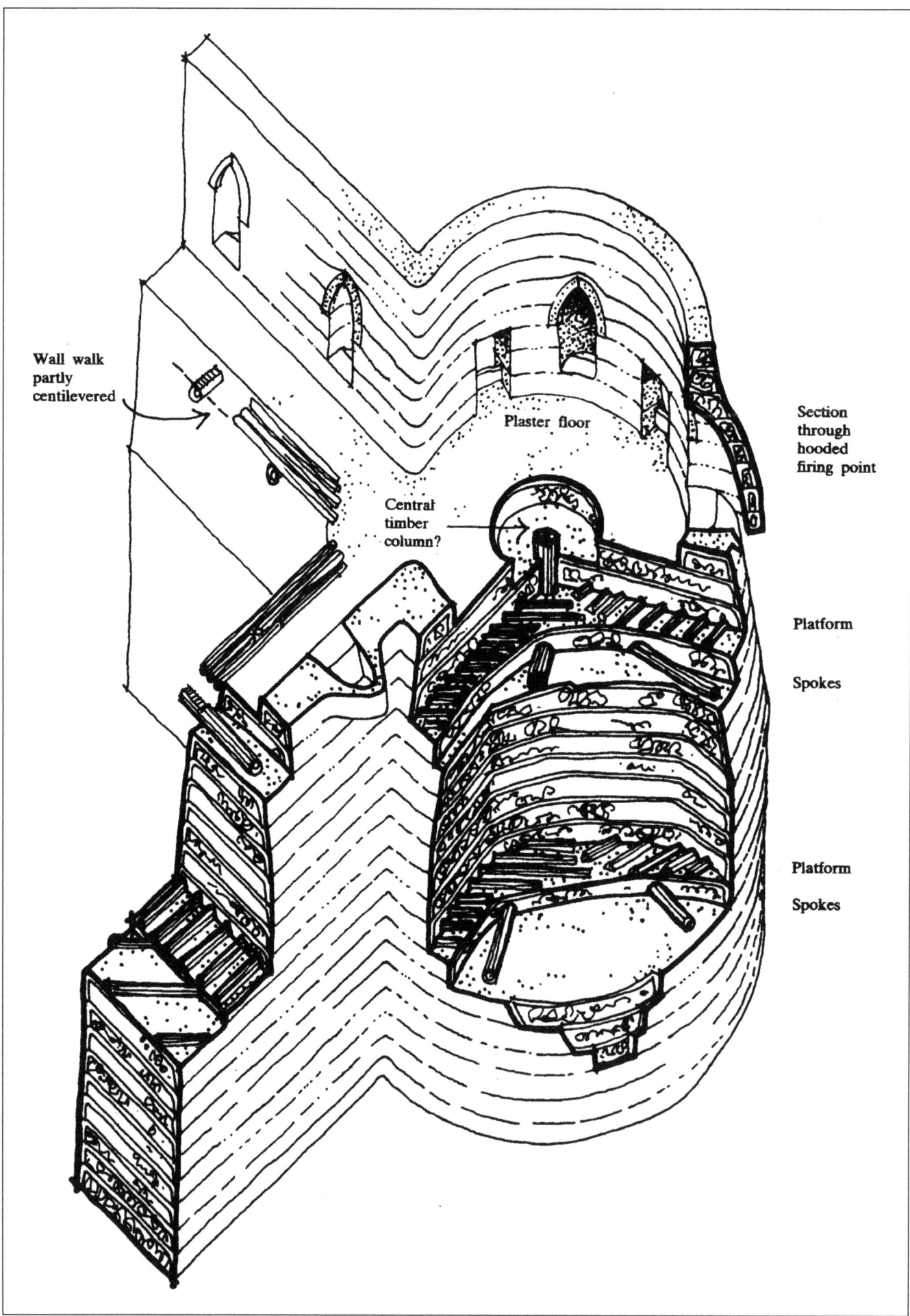

Fig. 6. Original construction of a bastion: inner fortifications

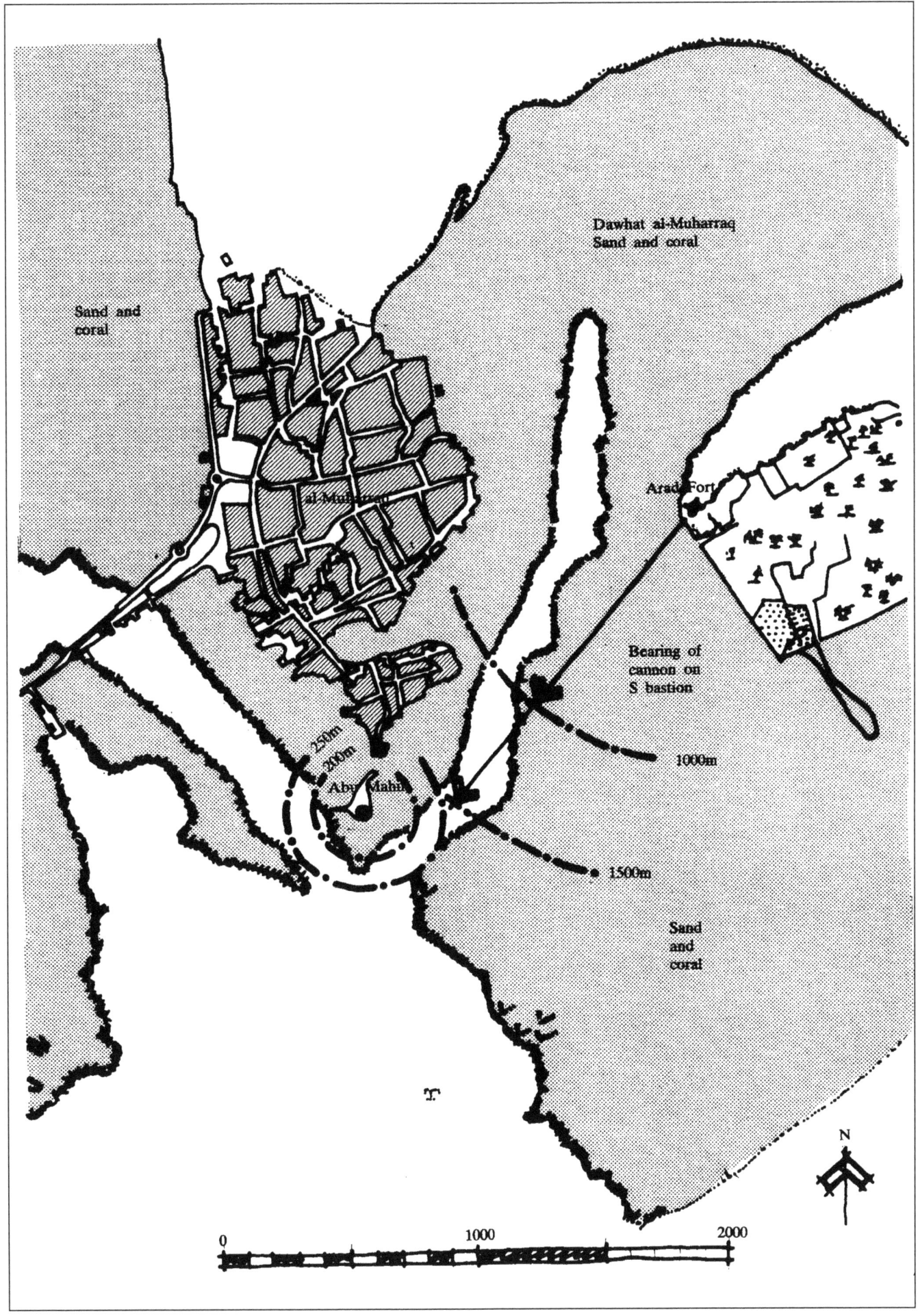

Fig. 7. The estuary and its channel: fields of fire

The Archaeology of Bahrain: The British Contribution

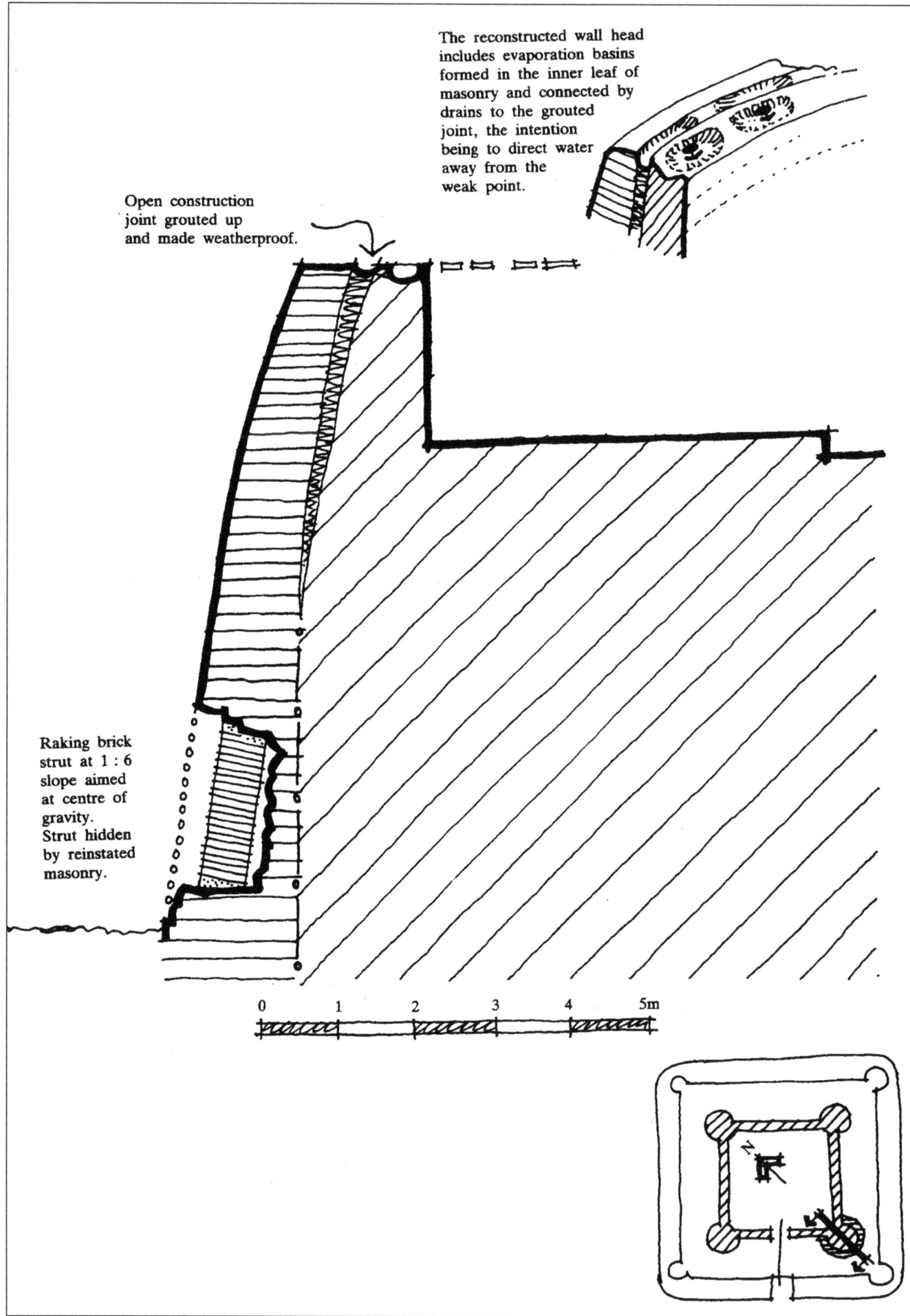

Fig. 8. Reconstruction of the south bastion

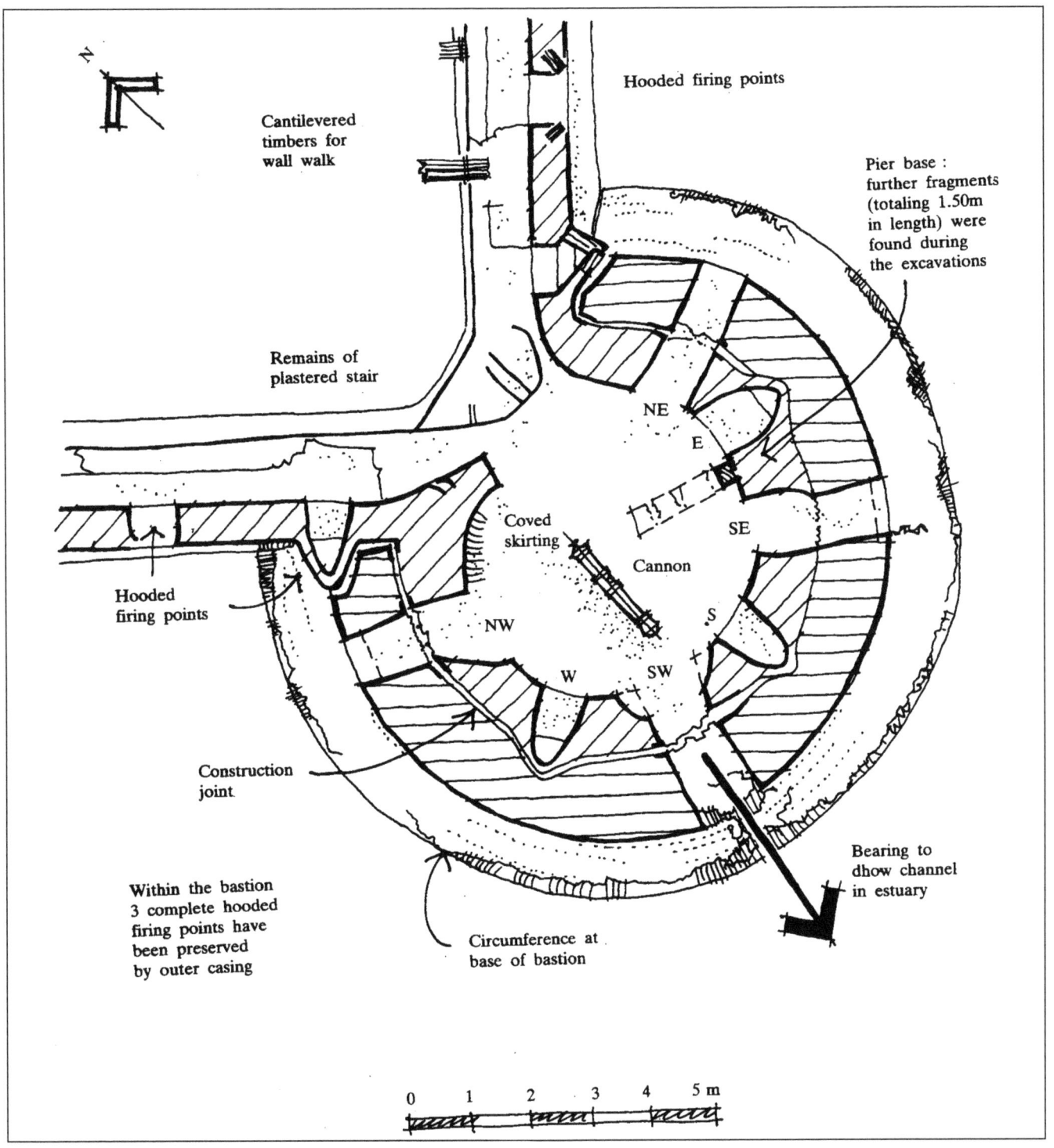

Fig. 9. South bastion: plan of upper areas

Artillery fire or rain did not cause the destruction of the wall heads of the towers and curtain walls, but the salts inherent in the building materials and the heavy dews which occur daily in Bahrain did. The water from the dew dissolves the salts on the surfaces of the building materials that are exposed to air, including the surfaces of voids hidden within the body of the structure. In the hot sun the water then evaporates producing new salt crystals that in turn attract and combine with other salt crystals and as they expand they lever off pieces of stone, mortar and render.[3] Arad is not a modern building constructed using washed sands. It is a traditional structure located close to the beach where there is sand aplenty albeit full of salts. In fact salt-laden building materials need not be a problem unless modern building techniques and materials are introduced, and at Arad I overcame this potential problem by either avoiding the use of modern materials, or, if this was impossible, by taking protective measures to isolate the new materials from the old.

---

[3] An example of the destructive power of dew water condensing even if not in contact with salts, was a tarmacadamed path through which ran a seemingly straight line cut with a circular saw. In fact this cut line lay directly below the edge of a corrugated tin roof and every morning, in the still Bahrain air, dew condensed on the roof and fell vertically on to the same spot eventually cutting into and through the tarmac.

Along the top of the extant walls and towers were the remains of what I have called "noses". These were protected points from which the defenders of Arad could fire at the enemy. The general form of the noses was provided by negative images at each end of the outer skin of the south tower where it had been built against two of the noses. Once I was able to clean away the sands from the firing platform of the south tower, complete examples of the noses were revealed projecting into the later outer protective skin. (Figs.9 & 6) The reconstruction of the noses along the top of the south west curtain wall was a relatively simple process for although the palm timbers forming the framework of the noses had vanished, they had of course left long holes where they extended back into the main wall. Thus, by inserting new timbers into these holes they naturally took the same angle and created the correct triangular base on which to reconstruct the noses. I thought it would be unsafe for the workmen to experiment with the reconstruction of the noses at high level, so we therefore first constructed a mock-up of a full size nose at ground level. This gave the men valuable experience, allowed me to think out any problems we encountered, and also gave my boss, H.E. Tariq Almoayed, the then Minister of Information, an understanding of what I was proposing to do.

The reconstructed height of the south-west or front curtain wall of the inner square was determined by that of the south and west towers. The wallheads of the three other walls of the inner square were consolidated but their heights were not increased in order to provide a record of the extent of the decay the fort has undergone. I think that had these walls been fully restored and built to the same height as the restored front wall, then the impression which visitors gain of Arad as an old fort might easily have been lost. On the other hand there were good political reasons behind the completion of the fort's front or south-west walls: the main reason was that from the airport road on the other side of Muharraq bay the fort looked complete and would therefore be viewed as one of the Ministry of Information's successful ventures.

The outer fortified square, its towers and moat

The walls and towers of the outer square were completely hidden by the accumulated sands so although their height could not be determined with any precision they provided archaeological evidence for a four phased history from original construction to eventual destruction.

However, despite the Portuguese drawing indicating that the outer walls were about the same height as the inner ones, any proposal to rebuild them would have been against my own philosophy of conservation. Nor would it have been possible or practical for two good reasons; there was no budget available for the work, and there was insufficient reclaimed sea-stone on the island with which to rebuild the walls and no new stone was available as it is now illegal to quarry sea-stone from the seabed. The decision I made was to build up the wall to just above head height along the southwest or front elevation. It is obvious that the original wall had been much taller, but taking the reconstructed wall up to two and a half metres in height at least gives a visitor the feeling of what it was like to be between the outer and inner fortified walls when they were complete. It also gives an idea of the chambered gate with its bench seats along the sidewalls on which the elders may have sat enjoying the cooling breezes that come off the sea during the day.[4] The other three walls of the outer square were kept low, at about chest height, to allow a to see the ground surrounding the fort.

Around the outside of the outer fortified square a plastered moat cut into the bedrock was discovered (see Fig.4) which had originally been filled with fresh water from the underground aquifer. Today the moat is empty because of over exploitation of the aquifers since the introduction of mechanical pumps that draw up water for gardens and washing cars at a far greater rate than the traditional method of camels or donkeys.

The moat was an exciting discovery, but of equal interest was the V-shaped design of the causeway in front of the main gate. (Fig 10) At times of trouble the causeway could be filled with water brought via a drain from the well at the centre of the inner fortified square. Imagine a team of attackers carrying a heavy palm tree as a battering ram, and starting to charge towards the door of the fort. Within two strides of arriving at the water filled causeway the first team member would be struggling with his knees under water and the impetuous of those behind him pushing him over. There would be chaos. If they changed their tactics and decided instead to walk across the causeway they would still have encountered problems. The bottom of the heavy timber doors was on a level with the battering ram, and in order for it to have any effect on the door it would need to be thrust upwards diminishing its effect as the men had first to overcome the weight of the battering ram when trying to hit the door.

The reconstruction of the entrance of the inner square

Despite the poor state of the entrance when we started work, there were traces of its original elements that allowed me to reconstruct it with confidence. There were impressions left by the palm trunk lintels, and the remnants of the reed reinforced pre-cast gypsum formers of the interior vault. When the sands filling the entrance were removed holes for the doors hinges were revealed, as well as a raised plastered floor and a drain below the floor of the entrance that was used to fill the causeway in times of trouble. (figs 11/12/ & 13/14)

---

4 At night the direction of the cooling breezes is reversed. They go towards the sea, as it is then warmer than the land and so convection currents raise up over the sea and this pulls the cooler air from the land. This change of direction of the cooling breezes is important, and even the builders of the apparently primitive barasti huts which are constructed of palm leaves and found along the coasts of the Arabian Gulf and Oman are orientated towards the sea to take advantage of these air movements.

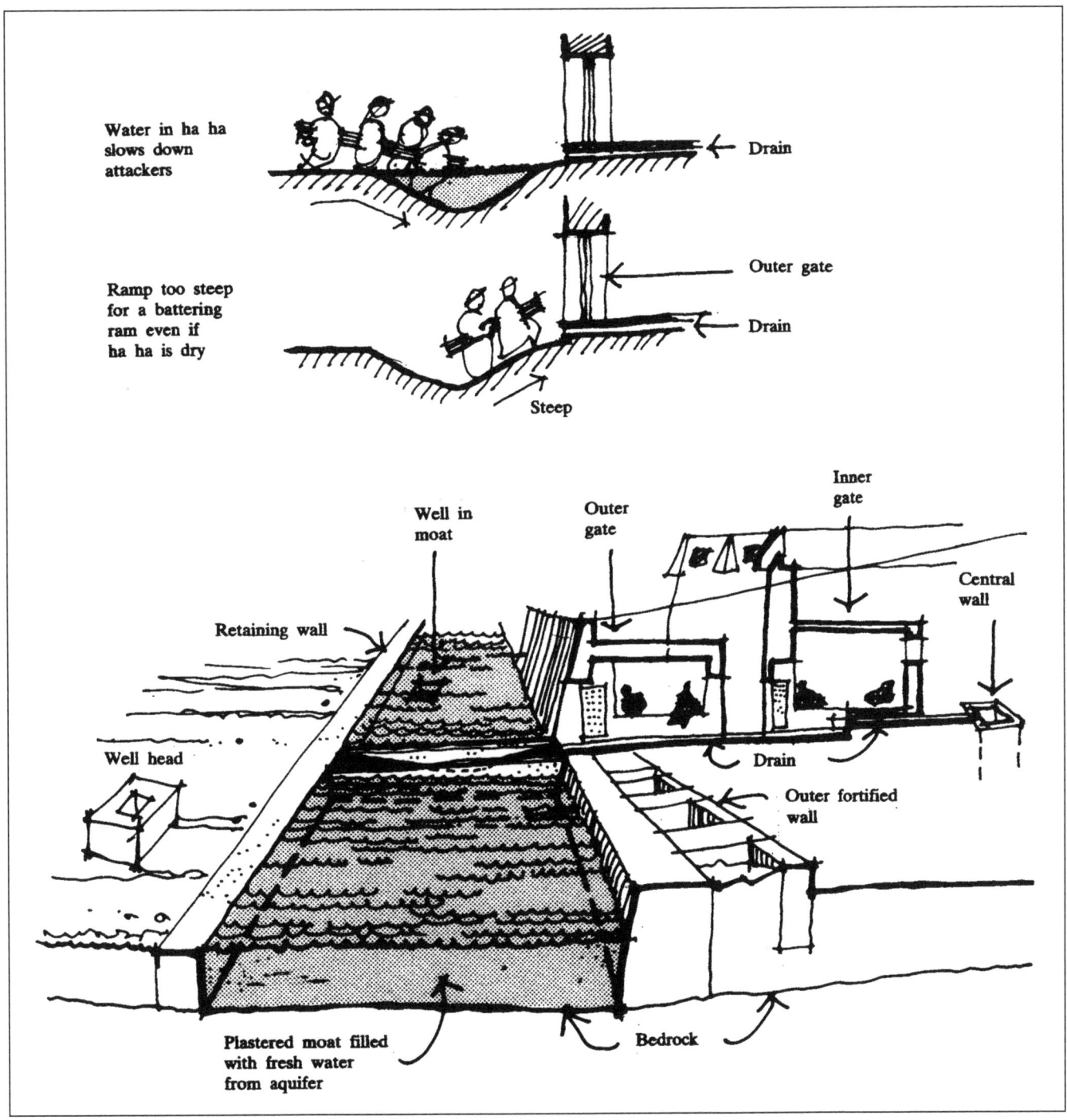

Fig. 10. sectional perspective showing the moat and the ramp

Construction techniques

The original building sequence of the walls was basically one rendered layer of masonry spiralling around the fort. Occasionally it was interrupted by inserted timbers or openings but the construction activity always took place along the top of the uppermost layer. As a result little, or no scaffolding was used and where, for example, there were arched openings the pre-cast reinforced gypsum formers could be erected in free air before infilling them with stones. This was all very logical, but restoration in a sense turns this logic upside down. The simple and elegant sequence of events no longer exists. Instead the restoration work must match and respond to the heights of the masonry and the rendered layers. The most difficult construction details to overcome are where the new work is founded on the top of an existing layer, and stability and structural integrity have to be created. Also where the work abuts the underside of existing material some form of structural continuity must be introduced. For example, having reconstructed the jambs to the entrance door to the level where the original lintels used to rest, it was far from easy to insert two new large palm trucks precisely into the impressions left by the original timbers, with restricted space between them and the extant masonry above. The operation was further complicated by the fact that this work had to be carried out by a team of twelve men working in a small space.

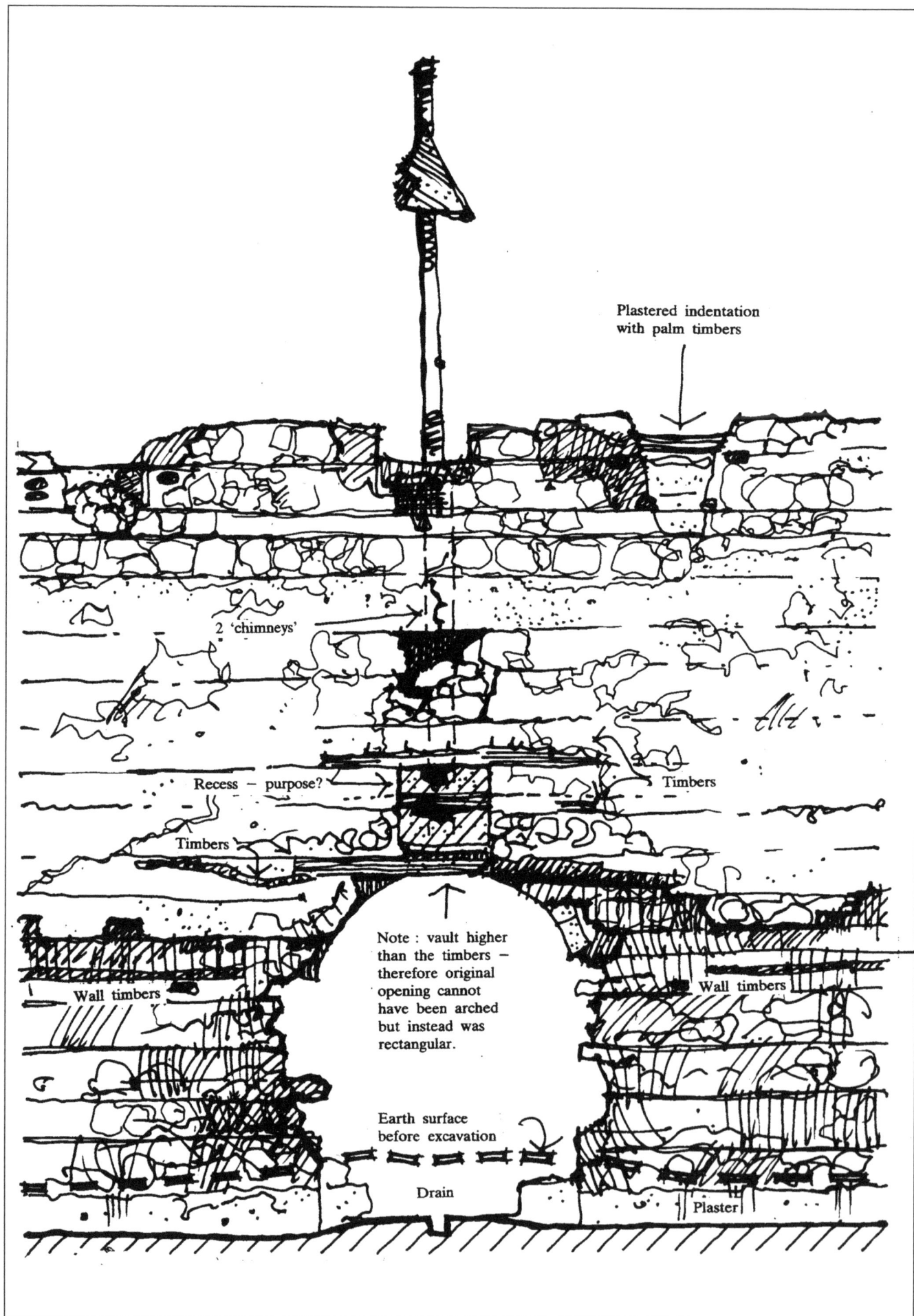

Fig. 11. Inner entrance: SW elevation

Fig. 12. Inner entrance: restored SW elevation

A similar reversal of the original construction sequence occurred when restoring the vault to the entrance, Figure 15 illustrates the steps we had to follow in order to reconstruct the reinforced arched gypsum elements forming the vault's skeleton. I have already referred to the fact that most of our materials were salvaged from our own excavations on site, and the reed reinforcement also came from the site as there are reed beds a short distance from the fort. Presumably the original reeds came from the same beds.

The strategic importance of Arad Fort

As already mentioned a cannon was discovered on top of the south tower that pointed directly to the entrance of the only navigable channel passing through the coral reefs to the safe anchorage of Muharraq bay.(see Fig.7) In order to check this alignment of cannon and navigable channel we went out in a friend's boat and found that if we deviated even slightly from the narrow channel we ran aground on the coral. The

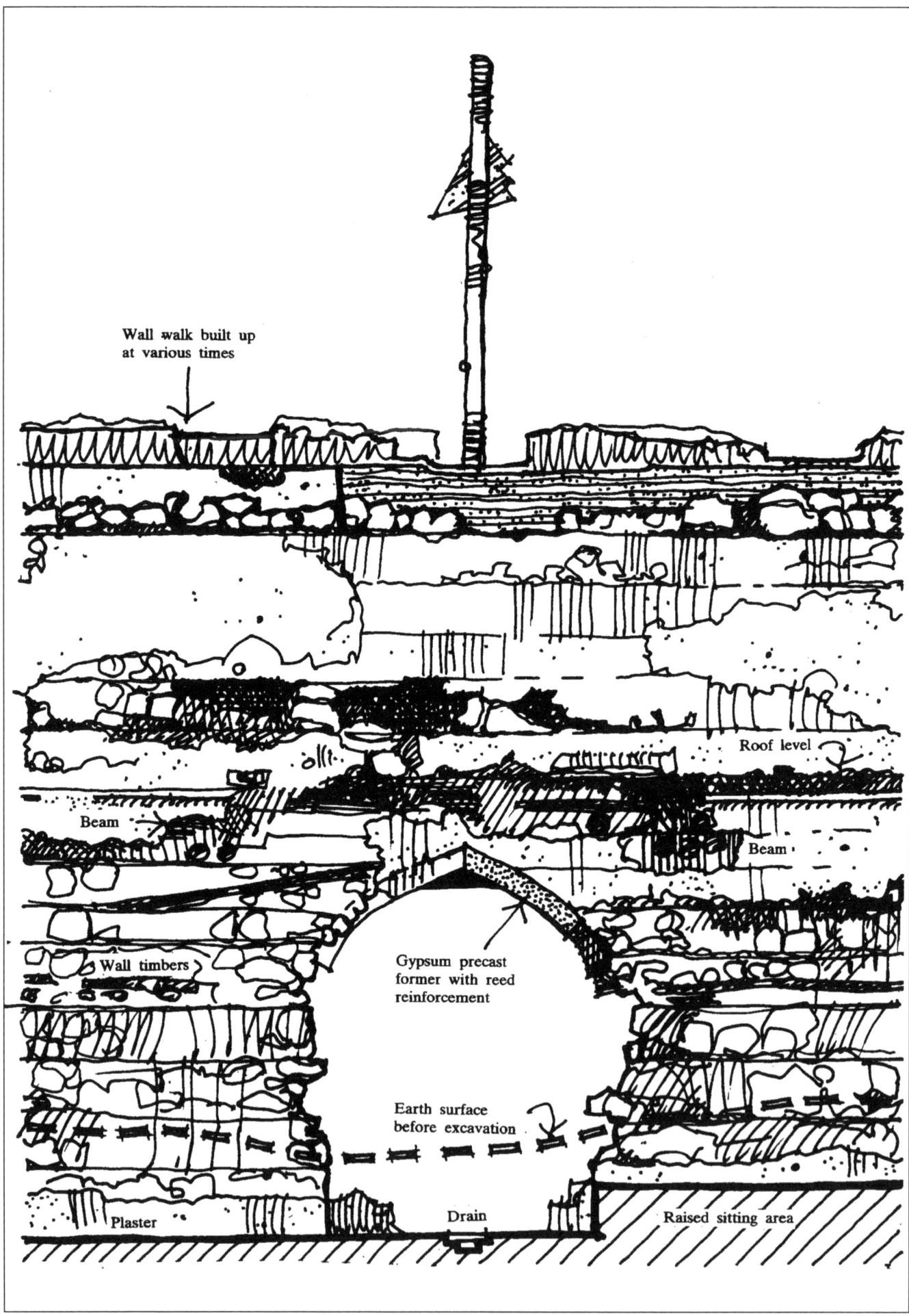

Fig. 13. Inner entrance NE elevation

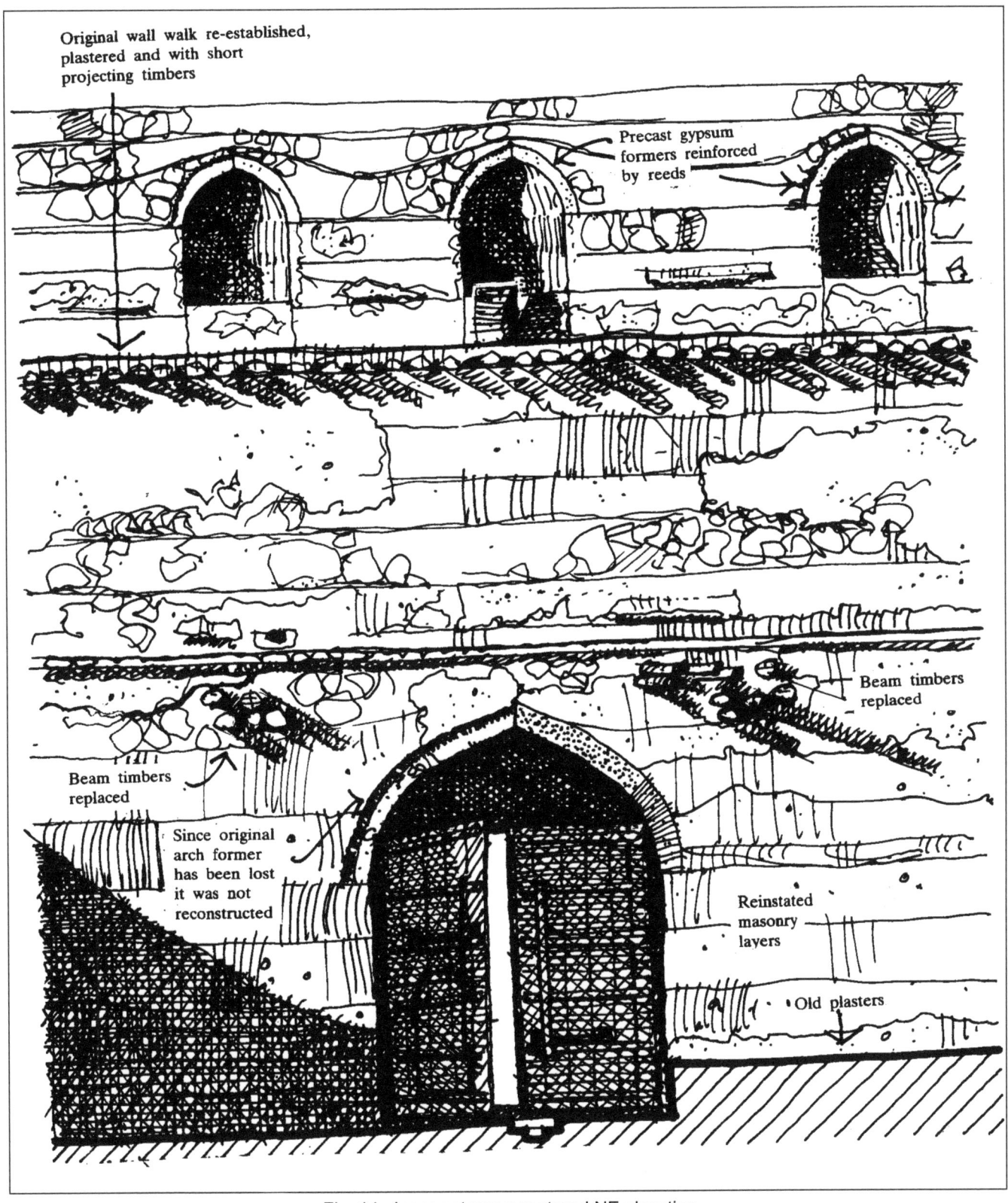

Fig. 14. Inner entrance: restored NE elevation

strategic importance of the location of Arad Fort, set well away from the deep sea channel separating Muharraq island from the main land, would therefore appear to be to defend the entrance to the anchorage adjacent to Muharraq. The deep sea channel was controlled already by another fort, Abu Mahir.[5] (see Fig.1)

Arad Fort's foreign relations[6]

I first encountered the layered technique while working in Oman during the 1970s. Since then through chance rather than design I have gradually put together a "gazetteer" of buildings exhibiting the technique. I am convinced that the

---

[5] The fortified tower of Abu Mahir is illustrated on the Portuguese drawing of c. 1635.

[6] At the Symposium I showed construction details taken from different buildings in different countries and using different materials, all of which

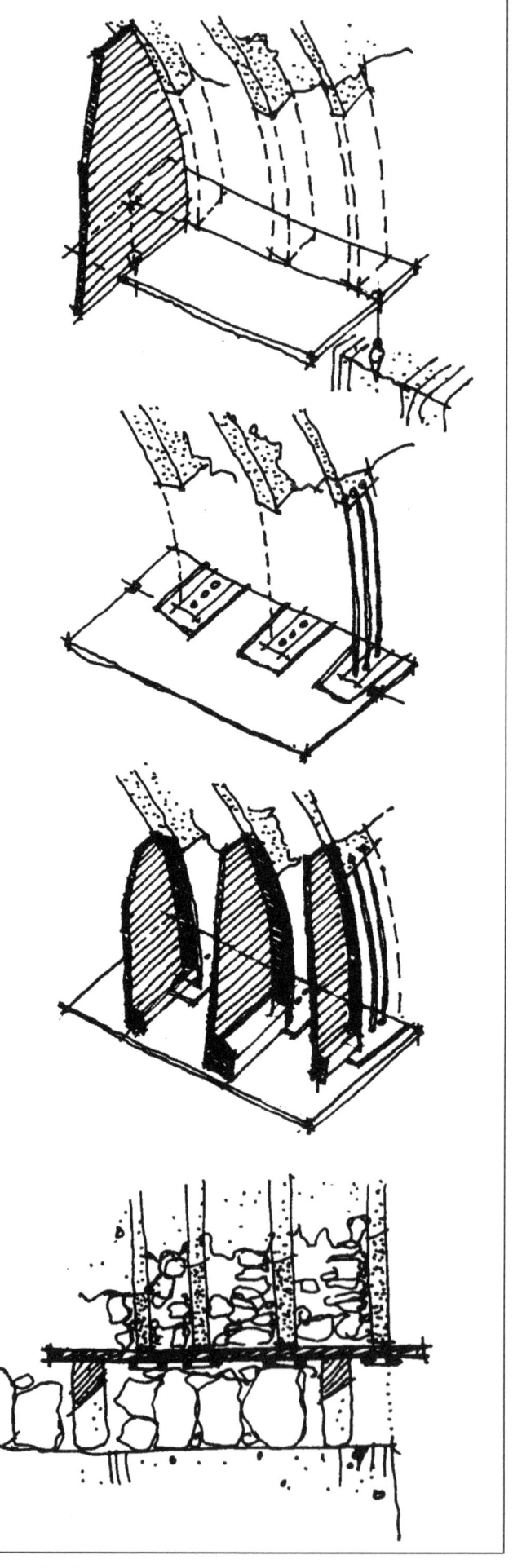

STEP ONE
Partly build up side wall. Construct ply platform set on gypsum pillars and level with vault springing. Plumb and mark wall face below. Make templates of the existing formers and extent them to meet springing.

STEP TWO
Mark the positions of the proposed bases and reeds. Cut around the marked bases, drill for reeds and prepare locks on the underside. Secure the reeds with glue, place them under compression to form required curve, screw up locks.

STEP THREE
Modify templates by adding to their curved edges pieces of two ply grooved and cut to the width of the formers. Reposition them against the existing formers and fix securely to the platform. Build up former in gypsum.

STEP FOUR
When the gypsum has set build between the formers. Remove templates. Partly build up the side wall below. Remove locks and platform, trim reed ends, knock out gypsum pillars, complete masonry layer below springing.

Fig. 15. The entrance vault: reconstruction sequence

layered technique is the indigenous construction method of the Arabian Desert and that the common thread linking all of the structures exhibiting the technique is the Arabian Desert. The structures are found from Anah on the Euphrates, at the northern limits of the desert, to Oman at its eastern limits. It is also found on the island of Zanzibar lying south of the Equator, and although its appearance on the Euphrates is understandable, its appearance in Zanzibar is surprising until one looks at its close maritime and political ties to Oman over hundreds of years. Zanzibar's first mosques were built nearly nine hundred years ago using the technique and even within the last hundred years many of the buildings and boundary walls of Zanzibar Stone Town have been built with the layered technique.

Further examples of this technique are as follows: in Iraq some 19th or early 20th century houses at Anah[7] which shortly after I saw them were flooded as part of a dam project; in Jordan, Kharanah (c 740 AD), a magnificent fort lying near the western extent of the desert, displays many architectural details characteristic of the technique such as pointed windows, reinforced arch formers and of course the rendered layers with a consistent height of 40 centimetres. Still in Jordan, and almost in view of Kharanah, is the famous Ummayad building of Qasr Amra, which I believe was constructed in the technique on the basis of the existence of the characteristic overlapping detail of layered renders. In Saudi Arabia there are many examples[8] including early 20th century Al Murrabba, King Abd el Azziz's palace complex in Riyadh.[9] Along the southern coast of the Arabian Gulf there are examples of towers constructed in the technique, which also display examples of the noses I reconstructed at Arad.

The northern part of Oman is filled with examples of forts and villages built following the technique: along the Batina coast north of Muscat; within and beyond the Jebel Akhdar, the mountainous range lying inland from the Batinah coast, and also southward into the Sharqiya. Within the Jebel Akhdar there is the large castle and town of Bahla, all of whose buildings are constructed in layered and rendered mud bricks and surrounded by a fortified wall of the same construction to enclose the communities' fields and imposing palm trees. There are other oasis settlements set around forts such as Samad which are constructed of layered and rendered mud bricks. At Bahla and at Samad are the only examples I have recorded of mud bricks shaped like sand castles as if turned out from a bucket. In each instance the brick is the full 40 centimetre height of the layer instead of the generally accepted three courses of brick to one layer. There are the famous forts of Jalali and Muranni guarding Muscat's harbour, which are layered and composed of stone and hard renders. Unfortunately for both forts their original layered renders of varying honey colours were covered up in the 1980s by the application of uniformly coloured flat renders. In my view this is a crime against two noble historic structures. It destroyed their external beauty and has the potential to destroy the integrity of the fabric if the wrong materials were mixed to create the new render. If, as I surmise, the render is not a traditional one, but one based on cement, it will inhibit the ability of the original materials to respond to changes in temperature and humidity. The result will be a breakdown of the core fabric behind the new renders. On the landward side of the Muscat guarding the city there are towers on every rocky, peak and where one of the wadis meets the city there is the small fort of Al-Rawiyan which has details seen in Kharanah in Jordan.[10] As has already been stated the technique is found in Zanzibar,[11] and although I have not visited the town, I suggest that some of the buildings of Lamu on the East African mainland also exhibit the layered technique.

I have found the chronology of the technique and the use and development of different materials as fascinating and surprising as the geographical spread. The use of this building method spans nearly three thousand years, and it is likely that there were a few extra centuries of development before that. The oldest example known to me is a wall dating to 800 BC, which can be seen at the Qala'at al-Bahrain, and was found in excavations carried out by the Danes. Incongruously, it is the most developed example found! The wall forms an entrance into a palace complex, and consists of ashlar masonry on its external face, and at the rear of each ashlar course several courses of smaller stones these are enveloped by a rendered layer that is a continuation of the mortar in the ashlar's bed joint.

Conclusion

By describing my restoration work at Arad Fort and the geographical spread of structures built using the technique, my hope is that those who are engaged in similar restoration projects, or in archaeological excavations in the region, become aware of the logic underlying the construction process and the individual details of architectural elements. The construction imposed a method of working on the original builders and when we are consolidating, restoring or adding to layered buildings we must bow to the same constraints.

---

conformed to the principals of the layered technique and many of which are almost identical despite being separated by vast distances across deserts and by age across the centuries. For the purposes of this written paper I have reduced the number of illustrations.

[7] I observed in the low rays of the early morning sun regularly spaced lines of salt crystals glinting like diamonds on what otherwise appeared to be a consistently applied coat of render but which was in fact a series of rendered layers 40 centimetres high. The reason for visiting Anah was to see Dr Michael Roaf's excavations there and although he disagreed with me I still consider that the walls of a mosque he was excavating showed layered characteristics.

[8] A perusal of Dr Geoffrey King's well illustrated book The Traditional Architecture of Saudi Arabia provides a number of examples of the layered technique.

[9] The remnants of the palace were recently restored as part of the new Saudi National Museum for which I acted as the mud brick consultant.

[10] These and other sites were identified and their layered construction analysed in Walls, A.G., Sultanate of Oman: Preservation of Monuments and Sites, UNDP and UNESCO, Paris 1978.

[11] Those sites identified as having the layered technique on the islands of Zanzibar and Tumbatu were referred to in Walls, A.G., *The National Heritage of Zanzibar: Its Future*, 1991, a report prepared for the Office of the President of Zanzibar and funded by the British Council.

Plate: Arad fort before (a) and after (b) restoration.

Bibliography

Afanas'ev G., Cleuziou S., Lukacs J., Tosi M. (eds.) 1996 *The Prehistory of Asia and Oceania.* XIII International Congress of Prehistoric and Protohostoric Sciences. Forli. Italia.

Al-Khalifa. Shaikha Haya Ali and Michael Rice (eds) 1986 *Bahrain Through the Ages: The Archaeology,* London

Al-Tikriti. Abdul Kader. 1975. Diraz excavation and its chronological position. *Dilmun* 8.16-20

Allchin R. and Allchin B. 1997 *South Asian Archaeology 1995.* USA, Science Publishers

Amiet,Pierre.1980. *La Glyptique Mésopotamienne Archa¿que* Paris

Andersen H.H. 1986 The Barbar Temple: stratigraphy, architecture and interpretation. In al-Khalifa and Rice 1986

Avanzini A. (ed.) 1997 *Profumi d'Arabia.* Pisa

Barreto de Resende. Pedro. 1635. *Livro do Estado da India Oriental.* Ms. Bibliotheque Nationale de France

Bent. J. Theodore. 1890, 'The Bahrein islands in the Persian Gulf', *Proceedings of the Royal Geographical Society* 12:1-19

Benton J. N. 1996 *Excavations at al-Sufouh: a Third Millennium Site in the Emirate of Dubai.* ABIEL I, Turnhout

Bibby. T.G. 1972 *Looking for Dilmun.* Pelican

Burrows. E.J. 1928 'Bahrain, Tilmun, Paradise' *Scriptura Sacra et Monumenta Orientis Antiqui, Pontifici Instituti Biblici,* Rome

de Cardi B. The Grave-Goods from Shimal Tomb 6 in Ras al-Khaimah, U.A.E. In Potts 1988

de Cardi B., Kennet D. and Stocks R.L. 1994 Five Thousand Years of Settlement at Khatt, UAE. In *PSAS* 24

Carter R. 1997a The Wadi Suq Period in Southeast Arabia: a reappraisal in the light of excavations at Kalba, UAE. In *PSAS, vol. 27*

Carter R.A. 1997b *Defining the Late Bronze Age in Southeast Arabia: ceramic evolution and settlement during the second millennium BC.* Thesis submitted to University College, London

Carter R.A. in press: Saar and its External Relations. Paper submitted to *AAE.*

Carter R.A. forthcoming *The Pottery of Saar,* Chapter in *The Dilmun Settlement at Saar: London-Bahrain Archaeological Expedition: Saar Excavation Reports III,* eds. Killick R. and Moon J.

Chakrabarti D.K. 1998 The Indus Civilization and the Arabian Gulf: an Indian point of view. In Phillips et al. 1998

Cleuziou S. 1981 Oman in the Early Second Millennium B.C. In Härtel 1981

Cleuziou S. 1992 The Oman Peninsula and the Indus Civilisation: a reassessment. In *Man and Environment vol. XVII*

Cleuziou S. and Berthoud T. 1980 Farming Communities of the Oman Peninsula and the Copper of Oman. In *JOS, vol. 6/2*

Cleuziou S. and Tosi M. 1989 The Southeastern Frontier of the Ancient Near East. In Frifelt and Sørensen 1989

Cleuziou S. and Tosi M. 1997 Evidence for the Use of Aromatics in the Early Bronze Age of Oman: Period III at RJ-2 (2300-2200). In Avanzini 1997

Connan J, Lombard P., Killick R., Højlund F, Salles J-F. and Khalaf A. 1998 The archaeological bitumens of Bahrain from the Early Dilmun period (c. 2200 BC) to the 16th century AD: a problem of sources and trade. In *AAE, vol.9*

Costa P.M. and Tosi M. (eds.) 1989 *Oman Studies: papers on the archaeology and history of Oman.* Rome, Ismeo

Costa P.M. and Wilkinson T.J. 1987 Settlement and Copper Exploitation in the Arja Area. In *JOS 9*

Crawford H.E.W. 1996 Dilmun, victim of world recession. In *PSAS, vol. 26*

Crawford H.E.W. 1998 *Dilmun and its Gulf Neighbours.* Cambridge, Cambridge University Press

Crawford, HEW 2000. Bahrain: Warehouse of the Gulf. *Traces of Paradise* 72-76.

Crawford H.E.W. 2001 *Early Dilmun Seals from Saar: Art and Commerce in Bronze Age Bahrain.* Ludlow, Archaeology International Ltd.

Crawford.H, Killick.R, J. Moon (eds.) 1997 *The Dilmun Temple at Saar. Bahrain and its archaeological inheritance.* London.

Crawford H.E.W. and al-Sindi K. 1995 A seal in the collections of the National Museum of Bahrain. In *AAE, vol. 6.*

Curtis J. 1988 *Bronze-Working Centres of Western Asia c. 1000-539 B.C.,* London and New York, Kegan Paul International

David H. 1996 Styles and Evolution: Soft stone vessels during the Bronze Age in the Oman peninsula. In *PSAS 26*

Dhavalikar M.K. 1997 Meluhha – The Land of Copper. In *South Asian Studies 13*

Driesch Angela von den and Manhart Henriette 2000.Fishbones from Al Markh, Bahrain in: M. Mashkour, A.M. Choyke, and F. Poplin (eds.), *Archaeozoology of the Near East* IV *Proceedings of the fourth international symposium on the archaeozoology of southwestern Asia and adjacent areas* (ARC Publicatie 32, Groningen, 2000) vol. B, pp. 50-67).

Drower. Margaret S. 1985, *Flinders Petrie: A Life in Archaeology,* London

Durand. Captain E.L 1879 *Notes on the Island of Bahrain and its Antiquities, as submitted from the Political Resident to the Foreign Department, Calcutta.*

Durand. Captain E.L. 1880 'Extracts from Report on the Islands and Antiquities of Bahrein' *Journal of the Royal Asiatic Society (New Series) 12*: 1-13.

During Caspers. E.C.L 1980 *The Bahrain Tumuli: An Illustrated Catalogue of Two Important Collections,* Uitgaven van het Nederlands Historisch-Archaeologisch Instituut te Istanbul 47.

During Caspers E.C.L. 1989 Some Remarks on Oman. In *PSAS, vol. 19*

During Caspers E.C.L. 1992 Intercultural/Mercantile Contacts between the Arabian Gulf and South Asia at the Close of the Third Millennium B.C. In *PSAS, vol. 22*

During Caspers E.C.L. 1994 Further evidence for "Central Asian" Materials from the Upper Gulf. In *JESHO, vol. XXXVII*

During Caspers E.C.L. 1996 Local MBAC materials in the Arabian Gulf and their manufacturers. In *PSAS, vol. 26*

Edens C. 1992 Dynamics of Trade in the Ancient Mesopotamian "World System". In *American Anthropologist, vol. 94: 1*

Edens C. 1993 Indus-Arabian Interaction during the Bronze Age. In Possehl 1993

Ehrich R.W. (ed.) 1992 *Chronologies in Old World Archaeology, Third Edition*, Chicago and London, University of Chicago Press

Frifelt K. 1975 On Prehistoric Settlement and Chronology of the Oman Peninsula. In *East and West, vol. 25*

Frifelt K. 1995 *The Island of Umm an-Nar vol. 2: The Third Millennium Settlement.* Moesgaard, Aarhus

Frifelt K. and Sørensen P. (eds.) 1989 *South Asian Archaeology 1985.* Scandinavian Institute of Asian Studies Occasional Papers No. 4, London, Curzon Press

Gadd. C.J. 1932 'Seals of Ancient Indian Style Found at Ur', *Proceedings of the British Academy* 18: 191-210

al-Gailani Werr L. 1986 Gulf (Dilmun) Style Cylinder Seals. In *PSAS, vol. 16*

Garnett.David ed. 1939. *The letters of T.E.Lawrence:* 136. London & Toronto.

Glassner J.J. 1989 Mesopotamian Textual Evidence on Magan/Makkan in the Late 3rd Millennium B.C. In Costa and Tosi 1989

Grave P., Potts D.T., Yassi N., Reade W. and Bailey G. 1996 Elemental Characteristics of Barbar ceramics from Tell Abraq. In *AAE vol. 7*

Hakemi A. 1997 *Shahdad: Archaeological Excavations of a Bronze Age Center in Iran.* Rome, Ismeo

Hakemi A. 1992 The Copper Smelting Furnaces of the Bronze Age in Shahdad. In Jarrige 1992.

Härtel H. (ed.) 1981 *South Asian Archaeology 1979.* Berlin: Dietrich Reimer Verlag

Hauptmann A., Weisgerber G. and Bachmann H.G. 1988 Early Copper Metallurgy in Oman. In Maddin 1988

Hauptmann A. 1985 *5000 Jahre Kupfer in Oman, Band 1: Die Entwicklung der Kupfermettalurgie vom 3. Jahrtausend bis zur Neuzeit.* Bochum, Deutches Bergbau-Museum

Højlund F. 1987 *Failaka/Dilmun: the Second Millennium Settlements, Volume 2: The Bronze Age Pottery.* Aarhus, Jutland Archaeological Society Publications XVII:2

Hojlund F, 1989. The Formation of the Dilmun State and the Amorite Tribes. *PSAS* 19: 45-59.

Højlund F, 2000. Qala'at al-Bahrain in the Bronze Age. *Traces of Paradise.* 59-62.

Højlund F. and Andersen H.H. 1994 *Qala'at al-Bahrain vol. 1: The Northern City Wall and the Islamic Fortress.* Jutland Archaeological Society Publications XXX: 1, Aarhus

Højlund F, and Andersen.H.H.1997. *Qala'at al-Bahrain 2 The Central Monumental Buildings.* JASPXXX: 2. Aarhus

Kennet D. and Velde C. 1995 Third and early second-millennium occupation at Nud Ziba, Khatt (U.A.E.). In *AAE 6*

Kenoyer J.M. 2000 Wealth and socioeconomic hierarchies of the Indus Valley Civilization. In Richards and Van Buren 2000.

al-Khalifa H.A. and Rice M. (eds.) 1986 *Bahrain through the Ages: the archaeology.* London, Routledge and Kegan Paul

Jarman,S. 1977. Bahrain Island: human skeletal material from the first millennium BC. *Bulletin of the Asia Institute of Pahlavi University (Shiraz)* pp. 19-40).

Jarrige C. (ed.) 1992 *South Asian Archaeology 1989.* Madison Wisconsin, Prehistory Press

Kervran. Monique. 1983. *Deux forteresses islamiques de la côte orientale de l'Arabie.* Proc. Seminar for Arabian Studies 13:1-77

King. Geoffrey. 19 The traditional architecture of Saudi Arabia

Kjaerum.Poul. 1983. *Failaka/Dilmun The second millennium settlements: the stamp and cylinder seals.* Jutland Archaeological Society Publications XVII:1 Moesgaard

Kohl P.L. 1979 The "World-Economy" of West Asia in the Third Millennium BC. In Taddei 1979

Konishi.M.A.1994. *Ain Umm es-Sujur. An interim report 1993/4.* Tokyo

Lahiri N. 1992 *The Archaeology of Indian Trade Routes Up to c. 200 BC: Resource Use, Resource Access and Lines of Communication.* Delhi, Oxford University Press

Larsen C. E. 1983 *Life and Land Use on the Bahrain Islands: the Geoarcheology of an Ancient Society.* University of Chicago Press

Lawrence.T.E.1939. *The letters.* ed. David Garnett. London & Toronto

Lombard P. 1999 *Bahrein: la civilisation des deux mers*: Catalogue for exhibition presented at l'Institut du Monde Arabe, Paris, 1999

Mackay. E. J, Harding. G.L. and F. Petrie 1929 '*Bahrein and Hemamieh*' Publications of the British School of Archaeology in Egypt, vol. 47

Maddin R. (ed.) 1988*The Beginning of the Use of Metals and Alloys.* Cambridge, MIT Press

Méry S. 1996 Ceramics and patterns of exchange across the Arabian Sea and the Persian Gulf in the Early Bronze Age. In Afanas'ev et al. 1996

Méry S. and Schneider G. 1996 Mesopotamian Pottery Wares in Eastern Arabia from the 5th to the 2nd Millennium BC: a Contribution of Archaeometry to the Economic history. In *PSAS 26*

Méry S., Phillips C. and Calvet Y. 1998 Dilmun pottery in Mesopotamia and Magan from the end of the 3rd and beginning of the 2nd Millennium B.C. In Phillips et al. 1998

Moon J., Farid S., Hicks A., Hicks M. and Kiely J. 1995 London-Bahrain Archaeological Expedition Excavations at Saar: 1993 Season. In *AAE 6*

Mortensen P. 1986 The Barbar Temple: its chronology and foreign relations reconsidered. In al-Khalifa and Rice 1986

Mughal M.R. 1992 Jhukar and the Late Harappan Cultural Mosaic of the Greater Indus Valley. In Jarrige 1992

Nielsen.V. 1958. Famed for its many pearls. *Kuml* 157-161

Oates. J et al. 1977. Seafaring merchants of Ur ? *Antiquity* 51. 221-234.

Oppenheim A. L. 1954 The Seafaring Merchants of Ur. In *Journal of the American Oriental Society, vol. 74*

Parpola A. and Koskikallio P. (eds.) 1994 *South Asian Archaeology 1993, vol. 2.* Suomalainen Tiedeakatemia, Helsinki

Peake H. 1928 The Copper Mountain of Magan. In *Antiquity, vol. II*

Petrie. W.M.F. 1917 *Ancient Egypt Pt. III*: 109-19.

Petrie. W.M.F. 1926 *Ancient Egypt Pt. IV*: 102-3

Petrie. W.M.F. 1939 *The Making of Egypt,*: 77, London

Pézard M. 1914 *Mission à Bender-Bouchir: documents archéologiques et épigraphiques.* Paris

Phillips, Fine Art Auctioneers and Valuers, 1987. Illustrated catalogue of a Sale held at Cornubia Hall, Par, Cornwall on Wednesday 16th September 1987: 39-43.

Phillips C.S., Potts D.T. and Searight S. (eds.) 1998 *Arabia and its Neighbours: Essays on Prehistorical and Historical Developments*, ABIEL II, Brepols

Possehl G.L. 1993 *Harappan Civilization: a recent perspective. Second Revised Edition*, New Delhi, American Institute of Indian Studies

Possehl G.L. 1996 Meluhha. In Reade 1996

Possehl G.L. 1997 Seafaring Merchants of Meluhha. In Allchin and Allchin 1997

Possehl G. L. and Rissman P.C. 1992 The Chronology of Prehistoric India: From Earliest Times to the Iron Age. In Ehrich 1992

Potts D.T. 1986 The Booty of Magan. In *Oriens Antiquus, vol. XXV*

Potts D.T. (ed.) 1988 *Araby the Blest: Studies in Arabian Archaeology*. Copenhagen, Tusculanum Press

Potts D.T. 1990a *The Arabian Gulf in Antiquity, vol. 1*. Oxford, Clarendon Press

Potts D.T. 1990b *A Prehistoric Mound in the Emirate of Umm al-Qaiwain, U.A.E. Excavations at Tell Abraq 1989*. Munksgaard, Copenhagen

Potts D.T. 1991 *Further excavations at Tell Abraq: The 1990 Season*. Munksgaard, Copenhagen

Potts D.T. 1992 Rethinking some aspects of trade in the Arabian Gulf. In *World Archaeology, vol. 24: 3*

Potts D.T. 1993a Four Seasons of Excavation at Tell Abraq (1989-1993). *PSAS 23*

Potts D.T. 1993b Tell Abraq and the Harappan Tradition in Southeast Arabia. In Possehl 1993

Potts D.T. 1994 South and Central Asian elements at Tell Abraq (Emirate of Umm an-Qaiwain, United Arab Emirates), c. 2200 BC - AD 400. In Parpola and Koskikallio 1994

Potts D.T. 1999 *The Archaeology of Elam: formation and transformation of an ancient Iranian state*. Cambridge University Press, Cambridge

Potts D.T. 2000 *Ancient Magan: the secrets of Tell Abraq*. Trident Press, London.

Potts T. 1994 *Mesopotamia and the East: An Archaeological and Historical Study of Foreign Relations ca. 3400-2000 BC*. Oxford University Committee for Archaeology Monograph 37

Prideaux. Captain F.B. 1912, 'The Sepulchral Tumuli of Bahrain' *Archaeological Survey of India, Annual Report 1908-1909:* 60-78

Rao S.R. 1985 *Lothal: a Harappan Port Town, vol. II*. Archaeological Survey of India, New Delhi

Rao S.R. 1986 Trade and cultural contacts between Bahrain and India in the third and second millennia B.C. In al-Khalifa and Rice 1986

Ratnagar S. 1994 Harappan Trade in its "World" Context. In *Man and Environment, vol. XIX*

Rawlinson. Major General Sir Henry Creswick 1880 'Notes on Captain Durand's Report on the Islands of Bahrein' *Journal of the Royal Asiatic Society (New Series) 12*:

Reade J. 1986 Commerce or Conquest: variations in the Mesopotamia-Dilmun relationship. In al-Khalifa and Rice 1986

Reade J. (ed.) 1996 *The Indian Ocean in Antiquity*. London, Kegan Paul International

Richards J. and Van Buren M. (eds.) 2000 *Order, legitimacy and wealth in ancient states*. Cambridge University Press.

Roaf. Michael. 1976. Excavations at al-Markh, Bahrain. *PSAS*. 6. 144-160.

Roaf. Michael and Jane Galbraith. 1994. Pottery and p-values: 'Seafaring merchants of Ur' re-examined. *Antiquity* 68. no.261. 770-783

Rowlands M. 1987 Centre and Periphery: a review of a concept. In Rowlands et al. 1987

Rowlands M, Larsen M. and Kristiansen K. (eds.) 1987 *Centre and Periphery in the Ancient World*. Cambridge University Press, Cambridge

Salvatori S. and Tosi M. 1997 Postscriptum: Some Reflections on Shahdad and its Place in the Bronze Age of Middle Asia. In Hakemi 1997

Srivastava K.M. 1991 *Madinat Hamad: Burial Mounds 1984-85*. Bahrain National Museum, Bahrain

Taddei M. (ed.) 1979 *South Asian Archaeology 1977*, Naples

Temple. Major R.1813. *Sixteen Views in the Persian Gulf taken in the years 1809\10, illustrative of the forces employed on the Expedition sent from Bombay under the command of Captain Wainwright of H.M.S. Chiffone and Lieut. Colonel Smith of H.M. 65th Regiment against the Arabian Pirates*. London.

al-Tikriti W.Y. 1985 The Archaeological Investigations on Ghanadha Island 1982-1984: Further Evidence for the Coastal Umm an-Nar Culture. *Archaeology in the United Arab Emirate vol. IV*

al-Tikriti W.Y. 1989 Umm an-Nar Culture in the Northern Emirates: third millennium BC tombs at Ajman. *Archaeology in the United Arab Emirates vol. V*

Tosi M. 1993 Harappan Civilisation beyond the Indian Subcontinent. In Possehl 1993

Traces of Paradise: The Archaeology of Bahrain 2400 BC to 300 AD. Catalogue of an exhibition held at the Musée du Monde Arabe and then at the Brunei Gallery, School of Oriental and African Studies London. 2nd ed. 2000.The Dilmun Committee

Vogt B. 1985 The Umm an-Nar Tomb at Hili North: a preliminary report on three seasons of excavation, 1982-1984. *Archaeology in the United Arab Emirates vol. IV*

Vogt B. 1994 *Asimah: An Account of a Two Months Rescue Excavation in the Mountains of Ras al-Khaimah, United Arab Emirates*. Dubai

Vogt B. 1996 Bronze Age Maritime Trade in the Indian Ocean: Harappan Traits on the Oman Peninsula. In Reade 1996

Walls.A.G. 1991. *The national heritage of Zanzibar: its future*. Report prepared for the office of the President of Zanzibar.

Walls.A.G. 1987. *Arad Fort, Bahrain: Its restoration, its history and defences*. Ministry of Information, State of Bahrain, 1987

Walls, A.G. *Sultanate of Oman: Preservation of Monuments and Sites*, UNDP and UNESCO, Paris 1978.

Weeks L. 1997 Prehistoric Metallurgy at Tell Abraq. In *AAE, vol. 8*

Weeks L. 1999 Lead isotope analyses from Tell Abraq, United Arab Emirates: new data regarding the 'tin problem' in Western Asia. In *Antiquity, vol. 73 no. 279*

Weeks L. 2000 *Pre-Islamic Metallurgy of the Gulf*. PhD thesis, Dept of Near Eastern Archaeology, University of Sydney.

Weisgerber G. 1986 Dilmun - a trading entrepôt: evidence from historical and archaeological sources. In al-Khalifa and Rice 1986

Weisgerber G. 1988 Oman: a Bronze-producing Centre during the 1st Half of the 1st Millennium BC. In Curtis 1988

Yener K.A. 2000 *The Domestication of Metals*. Culture and History of the Ancient Near East, Volume 4. Brill. Leiden, Boston, Köln.

Zarins J. 1989 Eastern Saudi Arabia and External Relations: selected ceramic, steatite and textual evidence, 3500-1900 BC. In Frifelt and Sørensen 1989

Postscript

This volume does not pretend to give an overview of the archaeology of Bahrain. It is merely a snapshot of one aspect of the work carried out over the last thirty years or so by one group of scholars. It takes no account, for example, of extremely important work done by Bahraini archaeologists. Archaeologists from the National museum have been active for many years now in retrieving artefacts and recording vital data, especially that from burial mounds, in advance of the massive expansion in housing which is an index of Bahrain's prosperity. Their professional skills are recognised throughout the Gulf region and many important objects can be seen in their national collections. There is now a pressing need for conservation and curatorial assistance so that these objects can be properly studied and displayed to full advantage in the magnificent National Museum.

Foreign scholars from countries other than Britain have also made a major contribution to understanding the history and archaeology of the islands. Without the work of Danish scholars little would be known of the famous Barbar temple or of the Qala'at al Bahrain, where more recent work has been undertaken by a French team under the direction of Dr Pierre Lombard who also put together the magnificent exhibition, first shown in Paris, which was the inspiration for the seminar at which the papers in this book were first given. The importance of this great site, perhaps the largest tell site in the Gulf, is shown by the fact that it is now actively being considered as a candidate for UNESCO's list of World Heritage sites. No doubt other Bahraini sites will follow and it is exciting news that work will shortly begin again at the Barbar temple where much still remains to be found.

Arab countries have also made important contributions, notably the work of a Jordanian team at Saar where in a joint operation with the Bahrainis they carried out the initial exploration of the settlement. More recently a Jordanian expedition has been working on the second grave complex near by

The British involvement in the archaeology of Bahrain is far from over, the academic links between our two countries are strong and will be further strengthened in this field by a new project led by Dr Timothy Insoll of Manchester University who is studying aspects of the early Islamic archaeology of the islands. This is a period which is so far little understood in the Gulf region and we look forward to new and important insights from this work. The government of Bahrain has shown great generosity in allowing the British, amongst others, to participate in the fascinating process of recreating the lost world of Dilmun and it is to be hoped that this fruitful cooperation will continue for many years to come.

Harriet Crawford

January 2002

www.ingramcontent.com/pod-product-compliance
Ingram Content Group UK Ltd.
Pitfield, Milton Keynes, MK11 3LW, UK
UKHW061213180426
11947UKWH00029B/2025